THE
GREAT WAR ILLUSTRATED
THE HOME FRONT

Other books by David Bilton and published by Pen & Sword Books:

Hull Pals
The Trench
The Home Front in the Great War
Oppy Wood
The German Army on the Western Front 1917–1918
The Germans on the Somme
The Germans at Arras
The Germans in Flanders 1914
The Germans in Flanders 1915–1916
The Germans in Flanders 1917–1918
The Central Powers on the Russian Front 1914–1918
Reading in the Great War 1914–1916
Reading in the Great War 1917–1919
Hull in the Great War
Call to Arms - Over By Christmas
The Home Front – Deepening Conflict
The Home Front – The Realization: Somme, Jutland and Verdun
Against the Tommies

THE
GREAT WAR ILLUSTRATED
THE HOME FRONT

The Realization - Somme, Jutland and Verdun

David Bilton

Pen & Sword
MILITARY

First published in Great Britain in 2016 by
PEN & SWORD MILITARY
an imprint of
Pen & Sword Books Ltd,
47 Church Street, Barnsley,
South Yorkshire.
S70 2AS

Copyright © David Bilton 2016

ISBN 978 1 47383 3 708

A CIP catalogue record for this book is available
from the British Library

Printed and bound in England by CPI Group (UK) Ltd, Croydon, CR0 4YY

Pen & Sword Books Ltd incorporates the imprints of
Pen & Sword Aviation, Pen & Sword Maritime,
Pen & Sword Military, Pen & Sword Select, Pen & Sword Military Classics,
Leo Cooper, Wharncliffe Local History

For a complete list of Pen & Sword titles please contact:
PEN & SWORD BOOKS LIMITED
47 Church Street, Barnsley, South Yorkshire, S70 2AS, England.
E-mail: enquiries@pen-and-sword.co.uk
Website: www.pen-and-sword.co.uk

Contents

Acknowledgements

As with previous books, a great big thank you to the staff of The Prince Consort's Library and Reading Central Library for their help, kindness and knowledge during the pre-writing stages of this book.

While some of the pictures come from books mentioned in the bibliography, many are from my own collection.

Introduction

This book is the third volume in a series that illustrates life on the Home Front during each year of the war. The many photographs show life through the eyes of those not on the military frontline. The book portrays the life of ordinary citizens and how they experienced the war. Important people appear only as part of the context of everyday life

This book is not solely about Britain; though the major part of it does record British life I have attempted to show the international commonality of various themes through illustrations from other Allied and enemy countries. Readers may be familiar with some, but most have not been published since the war, and others have never been published. As the photographs form the main focus of the book, I have quoted liberally from my previous books on the Home Front to provide the historical context using the experiences of Hull and Reading as typical but also to contrast experiences.

This is a book about the Home Front on an international scale. It is not chronological and, although themed, topics do cross over. Similarly, the difference between being in the forces and being on the Home Front can seem a grey area. It took a long time to train new recruits, and that training was done on the Home Front. In many areas, there were more people in uniform than out of it, a fact that became accepted as part of life.

What was the 'Home Front'? There are many interpretations of the phrase:

'the sphere of civilian activity in war'

'the civilian sector of a nation at war when its armed forces are in combat abroad'

'the name given to the part of the war that was not actively involved in the fighting but which was vital to it'

an 'informal term for the civilian populace of the nation at war as an active support system of their military. Military forces depend on "home front" civilian support services such as factories that build materiel to support the military front'

'life in Britain during the war itself'

All of these have elements of accuracy but none fully describe the range of experiences that shaped the Home Front.

For those caught in a Zeppelin raid, the Home Front became a war zone; it was not always 'All quiet on the Home Front' as assumed by the title of one history book. In this and the following volumes, I define the Home Front as the totality of the experience of the civilian population in a country affected, directly or indirectly, by the war. As there were considerable numbers of military personnel on the Home Front interacting with the civilian population, they too are included.

The Home Front was not a singular experience. Life in the countryside was different to that in the town or city, the latter being more quickly affected by change. In the same way, life in the Scottish Isles differed from that in the Kent countryside and people's lives in an East Coast town were unlike those on the West Coast. Of course the whole country experienced basic similarities but there were many factors that varied the war's effects. How could a family who lost their only son experience the same war as a neighbour with five serving sons who all returned? What similarities were there between the family of a conscientious objector and one whose father/husband had been killed? Or between an Irish family and a Welsh one?

While there is a common link between all of these examples, what links can be found between Belgian, French, Dutch, German, Japanese or Russian families? All these countries had a Home Front and all were directly affected by the war. There are some obvious differences. Neutral Holland was quickly affected by the war on its borders, and Japan, an isolated Allied Power, fought in the Pacific and escorted convoys to Europe but was otherwise largely unaffected. Both were unlike the other countries which, despite some differences, were all united by an invasion, long or short, of their Home Fronts.

We can add further layers to the civilian experience of the war through the Home Front. Neutral countries had to defend themselves against possible aggression and were on a war footing which inevitably affected civilian life. They were not at war, so nationals of the warring countries were free to move about as before the war and spying was rife. As safe havens, they became the guardians of hundreds of refugees or prisoners of war. And, as in the warring countries, commodities became short because their ships, once at sea, became targets.

Combatant countries on the continent experienced two types of Home Front, the obvious one being the civilians behind the fighting front. But in an occupied country, civilians were behind both sides of the line. All shared the same experience, but lived on the Home Front very differently, enduring different constraints.

This book therefore illustrates life on the Home Front for civilians on both sides of the wire.

The Home Fronts in 1916

A subdued Christmas quickly ran into the New Year. While restrictions meant that this celebration was muted, it was still full of expectation. Across Britain, and Europe, thoughts of the future were tinged with sadness of the past. 'The war has cast its shadow over all public and private activities during the year, affecting in innumerable ways our corporate and individual life. Few indeed are the families that have not one or more members in the Army or Navy, many of whom, alas! have laid down their lives for their country.'

Regardless, those that could, tried to enjoy New Year's Eve. Across the country people made the best of a poor situation. Taking Hull as a typical city, what merriment was available? 'The old year passed out in Hull quietly. The Humber ferry ran with difficulty because of the strong winds. Buzzers and sirens were forbidden under DORA. No church bells rung. Pubs closed at 9 p.m. The main topic of conversation was the loss of HMS *Natal* [sunk by an internal explosion in the Cromarty Firth on 30 December 1915]. Places of amusement were filled and there were numerous private parties. As midnight approached boys and girls filled the streets.' Fortunately the casualty list the next day was small.

'At the dawn of the New Year, probably the most singularly important aspect of the war for the government to deal with was the manpower shortage facing the army. Without men the army could not prosecute the war.' It was the same in Germany but there, there was no issue about compulsion. In order to increase the available manpower, later in the year Hindenburg demanded an Auxiliary Service Law. By the end of the year every male between the age of seventeen and sixty would be available for service.

'Before the war the idea of conscription had been seen as being totally against the British ideals of individual liberty but now it was no longer "the symbol of tyranny" but a necessary evil; without there would be insufficient recruits to replace the inevitable casualties of the coming offensives. In order to provide these recruits the government passed the Military Service Act on 4 January that became law on 27 January. By this act all voluntary enlistment, even for the Territorial Army ceased, and every male British subject between 18 and 41 years of age who (a) on 15 August 1915 was ordinarily resident in Great Britain (Ireland was excluded) and (b) on 2 November 1915 was unmarried or a widower without child or relative dependant on him, was deemed to have enlisted for general service in any unit as directed by the military authorities.'

By the end of January the report of the 1915 Lord Derby recruitment canvas was available, just a few days after the first men had been called for service. The results make for interesting reading. Below is the recruitment canvas for Reading, a typical medium sized town:

Men to be canvassed 8,263
Enlisted or offered 6,208*
Rejected on military grounds 3,000

*Breakdown

	Single	Married
Enlisted for immediate service	462	248
Enlisted for B Reserve	622	1218
Promised for immediate service	0	0
Promised for B Reserve	557	1132
Total promised or enlisted	1642	2597
Rejected by military	979	991
Total	629	3588

From 1915 unaccounted:

Foreigners	58
Dead or overage	90
Removals traced & details forwarded	198
Removals untraced	135
Total	481

Net unaccounted for – 1494 classed as follows:

	Total Number	
	Single	Married
Think unfit	223	185
War work, munitions, Marine & railways	59	78
Civil servants, Post Office employees, Police	11	51
Refused permission by employers	26	20
Unwilling:		
a) subject to conditions	27	103
b) No sufficient reason	213	498
Total	559	935
	16.1%	19.4%

'Provision was made for exemption on a number of grounds: being a member of an indispensable profession or trade or being trained or educated for that work; for serious hardship, financial or domestic if called up; for ill-health or infirmity; and for conscientious objections. To deal with the exemptions, the government set up tribunals. If a man preferred to serve in the Royal Navy, then the Admiralty had first call on his services.'

'Single men of groups 2 to 5 were called up on 25 January; with the others following in order (Group1 was the last) between then and 28 March. Class 1 to 13 followed this between 3 March and 28 March. Groups 24 to 46 were called up between 7 March and 13 June while Classes 24 to 46 were drafted quickly between 3 June and 24 June. This mass call-up had the potential to produce hundreds of thousands of new recruits but instead the net increase was just 43,000. There were 748,587 exemptions granted on top of the 1,433,827 who were already in reserved occupations or wore an official war work badge. More worryingly 93,000 men simply did not turn up when called. With the army in France 46,200 men short in April and 165,000 men below establishment at the end of the year, conscription was going to have to be applied with a less gentle hand.'

Obviously the system was not working in the way intended. Further changes were needed. So 'on 25 May the government extended the act to cover married men. The men about to be called up were "Derby Scheme" volunteers and in order to differentiate them from those who would later be conscripted, they were organised into year groups (as opposed to classes for those being involuntarily conscripted). The classes corresponded with their year of birth, Class 1 being 1875 and Class 23 being 1897, married men of the same ages were in Class 24 (1875) to 46 (1897).'

Enlistments through 1916

Year	Month	Total enlistments
	January	65,965
	February	98,629
	March	129,493
	April	106,908
	May	125,768
	June	156,386
1916	July	88,213
	August	111,771
	September	81,195
	October	97,684
	November	76,058
	December	52,005
	Total	1,190,075

When the conscription measures did not produce sufficient men, this caused disquiet among war workers because it meant that the government would soon begin the process of comb-out; taking those who could most easily be replaced by other labour. Throughout the war there were to be many comb-outs in attempts to provide sufficient manpower for the army. Worryingly for some was the implied threat on industrial relations. A comb-out could be 'used as a way of enforcing industrial peace with Trade Union members who were too militant, perhaps had promoted a strike or fostered any form of industrial discontent. They suddenly found themselves being called-up – their exemption counting for nought.'

With many men being drafted who did not want to serve but had to because of the law, there was considerable criticism of the final exemption from military service that allowed men whose personal principles did not allow them to support the war to go before a local tribunal to claim exemption. 'Predictably, this exemption became a burning issue. These "Conchies" or "Cuthberts" were, according to the popular press, "sickly idealists", "pasty faces", or worse and they suffered from a "fatty degeneration of the soul" and had as much pluck as a rabbit. According to the *Daily Express*, the term conscientious objectors was the new name for slackers, while the journal *John Bull* accused them of being a human toadstool which needed uprooting without further delay. In order to inflame opinion there were even reports of mock tribunals being set up to teach these "curs" all sorts of pious humbug in order to escape the drill sergeant.'

Feelings were so inflamed that even the Society of Friends, a body with profoundly pacifist beliefs, was attacked. It was alleged that they had totally ignored Christ's teachings on wealth and become one of the richest communities in Britain but were escaping the responsibilities of wealth by exaggerating the doctrine of non-resistance. However, there was another strand of opposition, the Socialists who believed in international brotherhood among working men. Meetings held to express their views were broken up by demonstrators who threw stink bombs and rushed the platform in order to close proceedings. Even the church seemed to be against them when a writer in the Anglican quarterly *The Optimist* suggested 'that the objector who in the name of conscience refused to fight was really supporting an immoral German militarism and should be exiled from the community he was defying.' Even academics gave the objectors little sympathy. In July, Bertrand Russell lost his position as lecturer in Logic and Mathematics at Trinity College, ostensibly as a consequence of his conviction under DORA for making statements calculated to prejudice recruiting. H. McLeod Innes wrote to Bertrand Russell on 11 July:

Dear Russell,

It is my duty to inform you that the following resolution was unanimously passed by the College Council today:

'That, since Mr. Russell has been convicted under the Defence of the Realm Act, and the conviction has been affirmed on appeal, he be removed from his lectureship in the College.'

Going before a tribunal a conscientious objector would be questioned by a group of local tradesmen and other worthy figures (generally elderly men), including a dominant soldier who was the spokesman and sometimes a woman. These bodies were notably inconsistent in their handling of the claimants, asking difficult and demanding questions such as whether they took exercise, whether they washed and what they did on Sundays. A favourite question was 'What would you do if a German attacked your mother or your sister?' The Bradford *Daily Telegraph* of 16 March 1916 contained the following from a Tribunal board:

Member: What would you do if a German attacked your mother?
Applicant: If possible I would get between the attacker and my
            Mother but under no circumstances would I take a life
            to save a life.
Member: If the only way to save your mother were to kill a
            German, would you still let him kill her?
Applicant: Yes.
Member: You ought to be shot.

There was little sympathy for such men and few exemptions on conscientious grounds were granted with most tribunals being guided by the government's promise to make the path of the conscientious objector a hard one. A further problem was that the act did not define what was meant by 'conscientious objection' so the interpretation was left to the individual members of the tribunal, and of course many of these were unsympathetic. There were also appeal tribunals, but most conscientious objectors fared little better with these. Even physically unfit objectors were drafted into the Non-Combatant Corps, despite their appeals, where they were made to do physical labour beyond their health. When their health broke down they could legitimately be refused a pension on the ground that their disability was not caused by war service.

A majority of the objectors agreed to assist the war effort in some form of non-combatant service like the Quaker ambulance units that had served on the Western Front since the start of the war (winning many medals for bravery), but those turned down were deemed to have enlisted. There were also those men who were termed 'absolutists' who refused to help in any way, who were also deemed to have enlisted. They could then be taken to a military camp where they were under military law. If they refused to obey a legal order they could be punished. If after being refused exemption they did not report for service they could be arrested as a deserter, handed over by the police to the military and be tried by court-martial in the same way as their fellow objectors who had refused to obey an order.

In total around 6,000 men were imprisoned and seventy died during their captivity. Mrs

Pankhurst recorded that those who refused to wear khaki and accept military training were bullied – one man was made to stand in a waterlogged pit for days, and terrorised and kept in handcuffs. Others were kept in dark punishment cells and given bread and water; if they went on hunger strike they were forcibly fed. Some were shipped to France where they would be classed as being on active service – disobeying an order on active service resulted in a death sentence rather than the prison sentence they would receive if in Britain. Shortly after their arrival these men were indeed sentenced to death. The pacifist Professor Murray found out and questioned Lord Derby who confirmed the sentences. Murray then contacted the Prime Minister who notified Field Marshal Haig that no executions must be carried out without the Cabinet's knowledge. Such excesses were classed as 'British Prussianism' by the No Conscription Fellowship and condemned by the *Daily News* which asked, 'Where are we drifting?'

With this sort of behaviour directed against them, the objectors won some sympathy. As if to confirm this, an Army Order of May decreed that henceforth such prisoners would be kept in civil prisons.

However, this was not an end to their suffering. The life they experienced in prison was not easy. After being court-martialled one conscientious objector was given a sentence of hard labour that meant that 'you had to spend the first month in solitary confinement with the exception of 40 minutes exercise, also you had to sleep on a bare wooden board without mattress.' Another, who had asked to join The Quaker War Victims Relief Work in France, was given 112 days imprisonment at Wormwood scrubs, including a number of weeks in solitary. After doing alternative civil service he was allowed to go to France to join the Friends Relief Service.

Six months later it was stated in the House of Commons that prisoners with conditions such as heart problems were being kept with venereal disease patients at Woolwich hospital where the sanitation was defective and there was no protection from infection.

Conscientious Objectors

Courts martial proceedings to 31/5/1919	8,806	
Courts martial proceedings scrutinised by Central Tribunal	5,808	
Men recommended to the Brace Committee for work of national importance under civil control	4,522	
Not so recommended	528	
Special recommendations and men who refused to plead their case before the Central Tribunal	748	Total 5,808
Number of men employed under the Brace Committee	4,126*	
Number of men who refused to work under Brace Committee	293	
Totally exempted after having been Courts-Martialled	82	
Agreed to return to the army from prison	10	
Medically unfit to be called up for work under the Brace Committee	10	
In prison awaiting work on the date 10th April 1919, when the Government authorised the discharge of conscientious objectors at work.	1	Total 4,522

* Of this number, 2,868 were subsequently sent out to Exceptional Employment, 27 died and 444 were arrested or recalled to the Army for absconding or for other breach of regulations. The earliest date on which any man was employed under the Brace Committee was 12 August, 1916. The last man in employment was released on 19 April, 1919.

The tribunals were not just for conscientious objectors, they were designed to see who was essential to the war effort at home and who was not. In essence the gave some members of the community the power of life and death over their fellow citizens. From the start they could do no right. 'If they spared the widow's son they were reviled by Lord Northcliffe. If they gave short shrift to scrimshankers they were guilty of dumping unassimilable dross into the Army. They were accused of robbing industry and of allowing industry to hoodwink them. They were attacked for browbeating conscientious objectors and for allowing themselves to be browbeaten by them.' The left-wing view of their activities was that 'nervous wrecks, semi-idiots and consumptives were forced by red-faced presidents of tribunals to get into khaki, and dragged out to France to die, cursing the country which had enslaved them in a military despotism and in whose service they had been forced to swear loyalty.' In reality the leniency of tribunals varied but there are many stories of strange applications and different decisions in different areas. While a tripe-dresser was sent into the army, a man who could kill, pluck and have a fowl ready for market in two minutes was indispensable to the war effort. Twenty-one single men working for Lord Northcliffe's Comic Cuts, Home Chat and Forget-Me-Not were granted exemption by the Southwark tribunal while in Croydon a woman had to plead to keep her final son (the other ten were serving) at home as her sole support. In Hull, an elderly infirm widow sought exemption for her son (an ex-regular who was time-expired and had served in France) as her only means of support because two of her sons had died so far in the war and her third son was crippled with a spinal injury. All over the country last sons were being exempted but only sons were not. There was also some evidence of class bias when 'at Huntingdon, a nurseryman stepped down from the bench to argue the case for his own exemption, which he was conditionally granted, and then ascended the bench again.'

There were no tribunals in Germany but there was still a shortage of men for the army. Like Britain and France there had been a great call-up of men, such that there were hardly any able-bodied males under forty-five not in uniform or employed in the mines, munitions or transport work.

Women, as in other combatant countries, were in great demand for war work. A visitor to Berlin noted that there were 'no men anywhere, women are doing everything'. In Essen, the Krupp factory employed 12,000 women, before the war it had employed none. By 1916 there were few jobs women were not doing. To make sure they could perform their new duties a network of women's welfare services was set up: war kitchens, day nurseries, kindergartens, leagues of housewives. A National Women's Service League aided 'soldier's wives or widows, and their families … to help ensure that they had adequate food.'

Manpower was not the only thing in short supply; most of the ordinary basics of life were becoming more expensive and more difficult to obtain. Calls for moderation in consumption in Hull, as across the country, had largely fallen on deaf ears. The object was to reduce imports but Board of Trade figures revealed the opposite had happened. Total food, drink and tobacco imported during 1915 cost £381,900,901, an increase over the previous year of £84,931,694. The largest contributor to the total was grain and flour, up £32,726,422.

Although there were fewer convictions for drunkenness, partly because of the no-treating order, alcohol was still a problem. Excessive consumption still affected production of essential materials. It was not just men: 'The women of Britain were taking to the bottle.' Initially the concern was that the wives of soldiers were squandering their separation allowances; then it was the newly affluent munitions workers. To avoid restrictions, women had taken to drinking at home and having 'tea parties' where the tea was alcoholic. But many women still went to the pub. This was shown by a census taken in North Paddington of four licensed houses. In just one hour on a Saturday night the clientele consisted of 122 servicemen, 1,361 male civilians and 1,946 women.

To reduce the time lost by alcohol-induced absence, the government ventured into the drinks trade with the 'Carlisle experiment'. The cordite factory started at Gretna in mid-1915 had attracted 15,000 labourers, mostly Irish, into a rural area incapable of housing or amusing them. They overran the surrounding villages and went into Carlisle by the hundreds. Although mostly well-behaved the rate of drunkenness quadrupled and there were complaints about what was happening in the partitions of the 'snug' bars. In response the government bought the local breweries and all the licensed properties, closing some of them, it withdrew grocers' licences to sell drink, brought in salaried managers, prohibited advertising alcohol, abolished 'snugs', and installed eating-rooms in the new 'model taverns'. Beer chasers were stopped and drinking under the age of eighteen was prohibited. The success of the experiment is shown by the change in one tavern and its extension into other areas. The Gretna Tavern, converted from a redundant post office, soon derived three-quarters of its income from food and in Enfield and Cromarty Firth the public houses were also nationalised. In Carlisle the experiment lasted until 1973.

Meanwhile in France, after the sacrifices made to save Verdun, the government decided to boost the nation's morale with a parade. On 14 July, National Fête-day 1916, a great inter-Allied march took place through Paris. Cheering crowds, eighteen deep on the boulevards, watched contingents from France, Belgium, Britain and Russia parade past and the President presenting decorations to the families of 500 deceased Frenchmen. Life in provincial France, according to a female reporter from *The Times*, was stagnant and automatic. It appeared as if life had come to a halt with the mobilisation. France and Paris were not the same, neither were the north and the south. To southerners it was a northern war, nothing to do with them except that they sent men to fight. It was distant.

 Parisian life, alongside the mourning and wounded men, was still extravagant and frivolous. Throughout the year there were outlandish fashion fads: small boys dressed as soldiers, little girls wearing policemen's cloaks and caps, women with short flared skirts, low cut blouses and high heels drawing the comment that they looked like 'shop-girls out on a spree'. Restaurants were filled nightly. This was made possible, even with a forty per cent increase in living costs, by the large profits made by war contractors, and the war-workers who shared a better standard of living. Much money was also spent on holidays, well away from the sound of the guns.

Back in England, following the pattern of 1915 the air raids started in January and continued through until the end of November. The 1916 season began with a small raid on the night of 22

January that resulted in one fatality, a raid the next night resulted in no casualties. A week later the air raids began in earnest. On the night of 31 January, nine airships took off to bomb the Midlands; weather conditions made navigation impossible and bombs were dropped on Stoke-on-Trent, Burton-on-Trent, Derby, Birmingham, Loughborough and a field near Holt. In all 379 bombs were dropped killing 71 and injuring 113.

One of the airships, L19, suffered engine trouble and dropped into the North Sea after being hit by Dutch gunfire over Ameland. On 3 February 'the trawler *King Stephen* came into Grimsby stating that at 7 am on the 2nd she had found L.19 floating, but in a sinking condition, 120 miles east of the Spurn Light. The Captain of the ship had implored the *King Stephen* to take the crew off, but the skipper had declined, fearing that his own small crew might be overpowered by the more numerous Germans [Captain Loewe and fifteen crew], and his steamer taken off to Germany.' The Captain of the trawler maintained that he searched for a British Naval vessel to aid the men but could not find one. As a result, all the Zeppelin crew died. Weeks and months later bottles containing messages from the airship were found in Swedish waters. The last message was dated 7 February and gave a different and accusatory version of the incident that provided the Germans with a propaganda opportunity they were quick to exploit. A second propaganda opportunity was provided by the Bishop of London who praised the skipper's behaviour and then went on to denounce the Zeppelin air crews as baby killers.

In 1916 there were to be a further thirty-five air raids spread out over most of England, resulting in considerable damage and a total of 272 civilians and 39 servicemen being killed. The Official History reached the conclusion that fortunately for Britain and the British people, 'the enemy authorities, having once committed themselves to Zeppelin warfare, failed to exploit it to the full.' Nevertheless the psychological effect of the raids was considerable. The airship menace was now assuming serious proportions and a massive reorganisation of the air defences was necessary.

By 16 February, the anti-aircraft role had been transferred from the Admiralty to the War Office and an air defence branch created, with the country being split into eight air-defence areas. With speed of communication being essential, telephonic equipment was used and every railway station and railway signal box was given facilities for instant communication.

Hull, as a major seaport, was a target more than most other cities. How did it fare? Hull's second air raid occurred on 5 March, only days after a table of predicted dates for raids by the 'baby killers'. The table was based on new moons which gave sufficient light for them to find their target. High winds, storms and other weather would affect the likelihood of a raid but could, of course, not be predicted. The periods when raids were likely were 30/1 – 8/2, 29/2 – 9/3, 29/3 – 7/4, 28/4 – 7/5, 28/5 – 3/6, 27/6 – 3/7, 27/7 – 3/8, 24/8 – 3/9, 24/9 – 3/10.

During the raid of 5/6 March two Zeppelins, L11 and L 14, hovered over the city for an hour. Their bombs caused extensive damage in the Queen Street and Collier Street areas, the glass roof of Paragon Station being destroyed. Seventeen people died and sixty were injured. Considerable damage was caused. *The Hull Daily Mail* said that the bombing 'destroyed houses, broke water mains, set fire to the Mariners' Alms houses, and to a shed on the docks. No guns or planes defended the town. The helpless population, in ugly mood, relieved its feelings by stoning a Royal Flying Corps vehicle in Hull, and a flying officer was mobbed in nearby Beverley.'

The next day, the *Mail* carried a special correspondent's report on the incident: 'Searchlights flashed across the sky. Two great beams...immediately "found" the visitor. Simultaneously guns were put in action, and shells were seen to burst with surprising rapidity all round the object, which, still held in the rays of the searchlights, gleamed like a yellowish incandescent mantle. Shells burst with blinding flashes...the airship descended quickly to a low altitude, rose again and suddenly made out to sea.'

On 8 March, *The Hull Daily Mail* reported on the inquests on fifteen victims, six men, four women and five children, casualties of 5 March. The coroner presumed that their deaths were caused by the 'atrocious air raid' which had taken placed the previous day. He said that 'all who had suffered would receive consideration. Provision would be made for proper burial, and those who had lost furniture would be recompensed. Everything possible would be done for those who had suffered.'

The stories told were very sad. The first witness, describing the death of her husband, told how the building fell on top of them. On scrambling out of the rubble she found her husband dead. A caretaker described how they had attempted to rescue an 89-year-old from the flames in his bedroom. Another inquest concerned three sisters. The bomb demolished most of their house leaving the father, who had been in bed, to find one of his daughters dead and the other two lying on the ground, fatally injured.

A pathetic story was told by a mother, the wife of a fish fryer, whose 8-year-old son was killed. She had taken him and other children into the street thinking it would be safer. However, while they were walking, they were hit by bomb fragments. They were all knocked down. She and one child got up; her son was dead.

A 63-year-old man was found under debris wrapped in bedclothes. He was killed in his sleep. A wife described how her husband had gone to find out whether the safety buzzer was likely to be sounded. After that she knew nothing about what happened to him.

An especially sad story was the death of a mother and her four children, two boys and two girls, aged eight, six, four and two. The bomb had levelled their house and only the father survived. In the Commons, the government expressed their sympathy with relatives of the killed.

In comparison, Paris experienced just one Zeppelin raid during the year. Twenty-four people were killed.

Showing any form of light after dark, for fear of guiding raiders to their targets, was prohibited by DORA regulations and strictly enforced by fines. Regulations also included no bonfires after dark, especially during an air raid alarm date. On Northgate in Cottingham, on the night of 1 April, Samuel Johnson, a labourer, failed to extinguish the bonfire at his cottage. For this oversight he was fined 15 shillings because it 'cast a reflection for a considerable distance'.

On the night of 5 April, Edward Sutton was fined 9s. His crime? Striking a match on the Ferriby Road before 10 o'clock on the night of an alarm. An attempted raid that night was not successful.

In the same session at the magistrates court, several breaches of the lighting orders, at Hessle, Cottingham, and elsewhere, were dealt with. Mrs Briggs of Hessle was fined 40s, William Jackson was fined 30s and William Harland and Thomas Smith were both fined 25s.

Sometimes it was a case of damned if you do and damned if you don't. Edward George, a Cottingham grocer, and a volunteer dispatch rider, rode his motor cycle, without lights, on the night of 5 April, under the orders of a Special Constable. As a result he collided with a cart. Fortunately the magistrate understood the regulations, and while he castigated the specials for issuing the orders, he respited judgement on payment of costs.

For most cities and towns there would be no raids but the threat was still there. Reading never experienced a raid but was prepared. Alderman Bull, Chairman of the Reading Watch Committee, 'made an important statement in regard to the precautions to be taken in the event of a Zeppelin raid'. When the alarm sounded, 'everyone should get under cover, and…the lights in private houses, shops and every other description of buildings should be extinguished, and only candles be used; also that the gas should be turned off at the meter and the electric lights at the switches.'

Although were no raids, there certainly were scares. After one incident, *The Reading Chronicle* reported that it was both a humorous and a nerve-wracking situation. It occurred at a time before most people had gone to bed and as a result some strange scenes were seen. Men left their games at the club unfinished and rushed off home. Tramcars dashed to the depot, leaving their erstwhile passengers to make their way home in the darkness. Business continued but by candlelight, to the great inconvenience of all. The worst hit were those travelling on the railway. 'For three-and-a-half hours…the passengers were confined to their lightless compartments.' The writer concluded by saying Reading should think itself lucky that the risk of a Zeppelin visit was extremely low.

In 1914, the lights had been merely screened against the sky but this method resulted in throwing pools of light on the roads. As time went by the level of blackout had improved but places like London could never be disguised because of the reflection of the river Thames and the Lea Valley reservoir (the lake in St James's Park had been drained early in the war to avoid this problem for central London). Some towns insisted on a complete blackout while others believed that the best protection lay in searchlights and artillery. Norwich had strict lighting regulations, so strict that men were fined for striking matches in the street to light their cigarettes or pipes.

In order to make sure citizens knew when vehicles needed to have lights on and when the town would be darkened, a simple table was printed in *The Reading Chronicle*, week by week:

Date	Vehicles to be lighted	Town to be darkened
January 10	4.40	5.40
January 11	4.42	5.42
January 12	4.43	5.43
January 13	4.44	5.44
January 14	4.45	5.45
January 15	4.46	5.46
January 16	4.48	5.48

There were concerns for safety, so guidance was provided. Pedestrians were urgently advised 'to walk on the path and not in the road as the amount of light allowed is insufficient to enable the driver to see a pedestrian at any appreciable distance, especially in country roads.' In many areas there were no footpaths; in such places the suggestion was that 'pedestrians should walk on the right side of the road so as to face the approaching traffic and avoid the risk of being overtaken by vehicles coming up from behind them.' It was pointed out that soldiers in uniform were particularly hard to see.

Naturally, insurance companies were quick to provide assistance. On the front page of the 1 January edition, *The Reading Standard* carried a large advert for insurance headed 'Darkened streets increase the risk of accidents.' The London Guarantee and Accident Co Ltd offered a special policy, for moderate payment, to provide substantial benefits for personal injury sustained in the streets (at any time of day or night), including accidents to or caused by vehicles.

Other aspects of lighting also caused problems. Throughout the war there were stories about car headlamps being used by enemy agents to direct the raiding airships over England. Both police and military authorities spent considerable amounts of time and manpower investigating each sighting. Only one case was brought to the point of prosecution but this was eventually dropped. As a result of this drastic orders for the reduction of motorcar lamps were enforced. Speeding trains gave off light from their funnels and from the railway carriages; as a result trains slowed down and in some cases services ceased. These measures were useful for defensive purposes but they also aided the enemy by their disruption to the flow of munitions. Even 'arcing' (intermittent flashes of light caused by faulty contact between pick-up arm and conductor-rail or wires) from trams caused a problem at night, reducing services, and on air raid nights many electric train and tram drivers refused to work 'so that measures had to be instituted to keep compulsory "slow-motion" services going, in order to evacuate the crowds attempting to leave any seemingly threatened area.'

During the first two years of the war it had been thought unnecessary to warn of impending air raids. However, as the number of munitions plants grew and had to be kept open twenty-four hours a day, it became necessary to have a warning in order to prevent workers from abandoning their factories. This need resulted in an air raid warning system with warning maroons and all-clear bugles. As well as advance warnings came better protection from artillery and searchlights and the formation of Home Defence Squadrons of the Royal Flying Corps with pilots trained and aerodromes prepared for night flying.

With such massively improved defences, the War Office, in the shape of the Royal Flying Corps, equipped with suitable planes and a new type of explosive ammunition, was now in the position to expose the vulnerability of the Zeppelin. On the night of 2 September, the largest airship raid of all was launched against London. Sixteen German Army and Navy Zeppelins carrying 460 bombs attempted to bomb the City of London but were met with bad weather and gunfire; little material damage was done and casualties were low (four dead and eight injured).

On 3 September 1916, airship SL11, commanded by London-born Hauptmann Schramm, was caught in the beams of two searchlights over north London that he was unable to shake off. The gunfire was more intense than ever before and although it was inaccurate the airship scattered its bombs on the Enfield, Ponders End, Tottenham, Edmonton and Finsbury Park districts, instead of on the City. Thousands watched as three pilots from 39 Squadron attacked, with Lieutenant Leefe Robinson in the forefront. After firing three drums of New Brock and Pomeroy ammunition into the airship the rear part of the craft started to burn. In a few seconds the whole airship was on fire and falling out of the sky. To the crowd below it was an unbelievable spectacle, regardless of whether people were burning to death inside. Before their eyes a tremendous fireball plunged to earth. A 9-year-old boy, remembering the experience sixty-four years later, recalled that the 'spontaneous barrage of cheering and shouting made the roar of a hundred thousand people at a pre-war Cup Final sound like an undertone. People danced, kissed, hugged and sang.' For this attack, Leefe Robinson was awarded the Victoria Cross.

Although any death in war is unfortunate, when the civilian death toll is put into perspective it was tiny. The raid on 3 September killed just two people. In *The Times* the next day, which described the destruction of the Zeppelin at Cuffley, were the names of 178 officers and 4,530 men killed or wounded on the Western Front.

The Zeppelin menace to London had effectively been mastered. However, in November a cheaper and more dangerous menace made its appearance – the bomber.

For everyone in the warring nations there were three constants: change, petty crime and death. Death did not come only to military personnel and civilians through enemy action, but also through disease, old age and suicide.

Of the latter, there were one successful and two unsuccessful attempts in Hull. John Keech and Aaron Clixby were charged in separate incidents for trying to cut their throats. No reason was given for their behaviour, and nothing other than an unsound mind could be determined for William Gray's suicide. The 53-year-old waggon inspector, employed by the Lancashire and Yorkshire Railway, who lived at 27 Cambridge Street, committed suicide by attaching a tube from the gas jet to his mouth. Although he had been out of work for six months, he had no financial problems and was not depressed. Complaining he could not sleep, he sent his wife to get a sleeping draught. On return she found him dead with a pipe in his mouth attached to the gas meter. Death was due to gas poisoning.

As for petty crimes, there were pig killers. In March, 12-year-old Joseph Barnes was accused of killing a pig and remanded because he had three previous convictions.

In Reading, as in Hull, there was little in the way of serious crime. William Norris was summoned for keeping a dog without a licence and admitted the offence. Fred Higgins, a Clyde soldier, had obviously not read the papers: he was 'summoned for not keeping burning a lamp so contrived as to render easily distinguishable every letter and figure on the identification plate on a motor car in Alexandra Road.' He was lucky. The case was dismissed and he was ordered to pay costs. Another soldier, Private John Symons, fell afoul of the law; he was charged with attempted suicide on 10 January. He had been found on the floor in a doorway in Broad Street, shivering and with a very weak pulse. There was an open razor in his hand. On inspection he was found to have superficial cuts to his cheeks and neck. When questioned, he could not say who he was. He was discharged and handed over to the military.

The third constant – change – could be taken on two levels: change caused by the war and the mounting restrictions and shortages; and the need for change to be put in collection boxes!

The most common method of collecting was the flag day. A successful flag day was good news and showed how generous the city was. The YMCA flag day at the end of March raised £693 3s 2d. However, after two years, although they continued to give, many were bored with flag days as a contemporary joke showed:

> Man: Oh! I'm sick of these flag days.
>
> Maid: Well I hope the soldiers won't get sick of fighting for you.

There were other ways of raising money and getting materials for those serving. One method was to ask for goods that soldiers could use. In Hull, one such Gift Day was an unqualified success. Gifts poured in all day at the Guildhall and Peel House and included donations of 184 tins of meat, 386 tins of fish, 35 tins of soup, 8 bottles of coffee, 51 tins of tooth powder, 88 tins of mints, 6 New Testaments, 224 tins of Vaseline, 9 boxes of bars of chocolate, 28 boxes of cigarettes, 10 boxes of tobacco, 33 boxes of matches, 2 packets of postcards, 2 writing pads, 3 hussifs (housewives – a small sewing kit) and cash totalling £23 14s 1d.

The majority of soldiers smoked so a great effort was put into keeping them in smokes. However, for many civilians giving to a tobacco fund was not a priority so some regiments experienced shortages of funds. The Royal Berkshire Regiment, like other regiments, constantly asked for donations to purchase tobacco. Short of money during the Somme offensive, while asking for money it felt able to boast of what it had achieved in 1916. Between 24 December and 10 July it had sent out 'nearly three millions of cigarettes, three-and-a-half tons of tobacco, 180,000 cigars, 2,000 pipes and 25,000 local papers' to the 7,000 men at the front. The lack of funds meant that no more papers would be sent out. Even with prizes, hand-made by men of 4 Battalion, such as a Royal Berks cap badge carved out of chalk blocks taken from a building on the Ypres front, they could only raise half the £800 needed.

The citizens of Reading obviously thought more of the YMCA than its local Tobacco Fund. In one day, the citizens gave £1,250 to the YMCA Hut flag day. The money was to provide huts that soldiers could use when on leave.

While the war in France was not going quite as planned, there were problems across Britain's other channel. At Easter, the Irish problem reared its head again, this time extremely violently. The rebellion broke out in Dublin and took a week to suppress. This was the signal that the great Anglo-Irish reconciliation brought about by the German threat had finally broken down. When the British government had introduced conscription they had excluded Ireland, making the point that this was not really their war. According to historian Trevor Wilson, the Easter Rising simply took this process of separation from Britain a step further. The German war offered the Republicans the chance to break away from Westminster completely. After many deaths and a number of executions the uprising was put down. While of great importance to Irish history it was a relatively minor occurrence in the history of the British Home Front.

In early June, the country suffered a major military loss when HMS *Hampshire* struck a German mine off the Orkney Isles while on a mission to Russia. The ship sank with the loss of nearly everyone on board. One of those lost was Lord Kitchener, Secretary of State for War. His death caused widespread shock and there were those who could not believe it was true, preferring to believe the rumour that it was a ruse to confuse the Germans.

From the start of the war there had been boycotts of musical works by German composers. Concerts were purged of Beethoven, Strauss and Wagner but they eventually returned, much to the chagrin of some. The Vicar of Netherton complained that 'the Dead March from Saul was unsuitable for a memorial service to Kitchener, the greatest Englishman who ever lived.'

In January the government had decided to close down German-owned businesses. The owner of Sanatogen was a German living in Germany who had applied to have the company become an English company. This had been refused and steps were taken to stop profits reaching Germany.

In May the business was wound up and bought by Lord Rhondda for £360,000. At the same time Bechstein, the piano makers, was bought by Debenhams and Bechstein Hall was renamed Wigmore Hall.

A further problem faced the government in the form of worker unrest. Lloyd George blamed the problem on the conditions of work, their subjection to new disciplines, the loss of prized rights and privileges, the shifting of workers from their homes to often inadequate accommodation, and a sense that, despite high wages, they were really only working to enrich their employers. When 15,000 Liverpool dockers, 20,000 munitions workers in Glasgow and 30,000 jute workers at Dundee walked out the unrest had turned into strikes. Lord Sandhurst blamed the problem squarely on the shoulders of the younger worker who he felt cared little about the war and thought of it only in terms of his own financial rewards. However, later in the year Lloyd George was able to report to the House of Commons a massive increase in munitions output. Taking two examples as illustrations, the annual production of 18-pounder shells (1914-15) was now being made every three weeks and of heavy shells every four days. And although there had been considerable unrest, affecting 284,000 workers in 581 disputes, these were the lowest figures since 1907.

In Germany, the Burgfrieden (civil truce) proclaimed in 1914 was over. Voices spoke out against the war and strikes, previously very few, now increased and members of parliament voted against the government. Anti-war sentiment was increasing and at a mass peace meeting in Frankfurt on 1 October, '30,000 workers passed a resolution demanding peace on the basis of the status quo' but this did not mean they wanted Germany to be beaten.

The change to a war footing was felt in most industries. As the demand for peacetime products died, factories switched over to war work. 'Jewellers abandoned their craftsmanship and the fashioning of gold and silver ornaments for the production of anti-gas apparatus and other war material; old-fashioned firms noted for their art productions…turned to the manufacture of an intricate kind of hand grenade. Cycle-makers turned their activities to fuses and shells; world famous pen-makers adapted their machines to the manufacture of cartridge clips; and railway carriage companies launched out with artillery, wagons, limbers, tanks and aeroplanes; and the chemical works devoted their energies to the production of the deadly TNT.'

In 1916 a lack of skilled men was already having a marked effect on dilution and female employment before conscription: with its advent many more women would be needed. By August, 766,000 women were replacing men in various forms of civil employment. There were a further 340,000 employed in munitions and War Office establishments. In February the government had called for 400,000 women to assist in agriculture and in March the Home Office and the Board of Trade asked employers to organise their work so that women could replace called-up men. By the end of the year women were seen doing most of the jobs that had previously been the sole preserve of men, for example driving cars, or collecting tickets on the underground. Women replaced men in the London Clubs and on the doors of the big hotels; there were 'conductorettes' on the buses and even women police.

It was the same in France. Rural areas were being denuded of men by the army, many of whom would not return, and the factories provided well-paid employment. Older men and women took their sons' places on farms. In the cities and towns fit young civilians were a rarity especially as the 1917 class had been called up a year early to replace the losses of Verdun. As in Britain, women stepped up to take their place. More and more male jobs were given to women, especially when the comb-out continued throughout the year. Indeed by November the only men left in munitions factories were those employed on work considered too heavy for women.

Women workers faced many hardships and dangers as they replaced men in industry. The varnish used on aeroplane wings produced toxic fumes and it was common for them to be found lying ill or unconscious outside the workshop; and the TNT used in artillery shells turned their skin yellow, gaining them the nickname 'canaries'. During 1916, 181 'munitionettes' were diagnosed as having toxic jaundice as a result of working with TNT, from which 52 died in 1916. In 1917 there were 189 cases, with 44 fatalities and in 1918 there were 34 diagnosed of which 10 died.

To look after this new army of workers a Female Labour Committee was set up. It provided more crèches and saw to the care of pregnant women. Night work was forbidden to those under 18, and only allowed for 18 to 21-year-olds temporarily and in exceptional circumstances. Inspectors enforced the rules. Women were now being accepted more willingly by industrialists.

More dangerous still were 'the monkey machines', in which a heavy weight was dropped to compress explosive into shell cases. Death at work was not an unusual occurrence under such conditions but it did not stop work. A story is told of one of Lloyd George's representatives arriving at a factory where just before his arrival there had been an accident. An explosion had killed four women who had been screwing shell fuses in place. He found work in progress in the bloodstained hut just as normal. Sylvia Pankhurst recorded a similar situation when a group of women asked to see round a National Factory prior to starting work:

'The workers wore rubber gloves, mobcaps, respirators, and leggings. Their faces were coated with flour and starch, to protect them from the TNT dust. Yet in spite of these precautions their skin was yellow. They asked the manager whether the work was dangerous. He answered: "Not so very dangerous". They questioned the women workers, but they whispered they dare not speak of their conditions… A few days later the factory was blown up. Thirty-nine people, including the manager, were killed.'

For the first time, many working class women were independent, not only because there were fewer men but also because of the higher level of wages they were earning. They spent their money on things previously only dreamt about, furs, fancy night gowns, make-up, powder and silk stockings. Skirts were shorter, trousers were worn and many felt able to smoke in public. In contrast to this, it was now the fashion for middle class women to dress plainly. However, for many of the wealthy the war brought little change, they attended the fashionable events dressed as they had before the war.

Increased working class prosperity was also evident in one unusual purchase, a piano. The editor of the *Daily Express,* R.D. Blumenfeld, noted that 'British piano dealers have never been so prosperous as they are today. You cannot buy a cheap piano for immediate delivery.' Some workers were also buying the best cuts of meat.

As a result of this increased prosperity, the fact that life went on much as normal, and because most on the Home Front were removed from the dangers faced by those fighting, a gulf developed between them and the men at the front who began to feel like 'strangers in their own land'.

German workers were not enjoying the same level of prosperity. Although like Britain and France wages had risen, price rises had had a negative effect. 'Average daily real wages fell by nearly 22% between March 1914 and September 1916, while the real wages of workers in the civilian industries dropped by 42% in the same period. This loss of purchasing power, together with growing food scarcity' was the cause of considerable discontent. The shortage of manpower gave workers the ability to make their grievances felt and industrial grievances increased. One of the most serious strikes, in which 55,000 Berlin workers stopped work for three days, was political. They were demonstrating against the sentencing of Liebknecht for his anti-war views. 'Equally significant were the Ruhr coal mines strikes that occurred in August, whose immediate cause was food shortage and then failure of wages to keep up with prices.'

For most Britons the war was becoming a way of life and its impact was noticeable everywhere. In February, for the hours between sunset and sunrise, the striking and chiming of public clocks (including Big Ben) was prohibited, followed by a ban on whistling for cabs between 10pm and 7am. Both the Whitsun and August Bank holidays were cancelled to increase munitions output, the later cancellation resulted in Hull dockers refusing to work unless they received holiday rates of pay. There were fewer arrests for drunkenness but at the same time there was an increase in the use of cocaine; to reduce this it was necessary to prohibit its import except under licence. Newspapers became thinner due to paper shortages while the casualty lists grew longer. Matches became difficult to buy. Luxuries like restaurant cars disappeared and top hats disappeared because they would not fit in to the forms of transport left to the public. Lack of fuel reduced the number of cars and postal deliveries became less reliable due to a lack of workers. The statues in London and the tombs in Westminster Abbey were covered in sandbags to protect them against bomb damage. There was an increase in spiritualism by bereaved mothers and wives trying to get in touch with dead sons and husbands. Tramps, according to a police report, had disappeared from the scene, being either employed or in the army. Even 'Guy Fawkes' night was banned, courtesy of DORA.

One change that is still with us was the invention of William Willet, a master-builder in London. Originally rejected as the idea of a crank, his idea of advancing the clock by one hour in the summer was accepted in 1916, becoming British Summer Time. Some objected, but the idea had much to commend it, giving an extra hour of daylight in the summer months and reducing the need for artificial light.

As well as a housing shortage there were inevitable price rises; the cost of food increased throughout the year. A poor potato harvest caused their price to double over the period from April to the end of the year. A 4lb loaf had risen from around 6d at the start of the war to 10d at the end of 1916. Butter and milk increased by 100 per cent during the year. Sugar, which was becoming ever more difficult to get hold of, also showed a 100 per cent price rise. The average increase in the retail price of the principal articles of food between July 1914 and September 1916 was 65 per cent.

Prices had risen but in Britain and France there was, as yet, no shortage of food. Parisian restaurants continued to serve food that was 'quite excellent' with the only limitation being the restriction to two courses. However, like Britain changes were occurring and more would follow. Sugar became scarce because of shipping shortages from the West Indies and the domestic sugar beet crop languished because of a shortage of skilled men to mend machines. This in turn impacted on alcohol production, especially champagne, which was also hit by a lack of skilled workers. Cheese and butter output was hardly affected because women replaced men in the factories. However, by autumn, with shortages caused by a poor harvest, queues began to form. Restrictions followed. The first was the introduction of National Bread: less refined, less white and less imported flour. The government introduced meatless days. The long baton roll was banned along with ices, sweets and chocolate sweets, although a chocolate bar could still be purchased.

Fabric prices had doubled and footwear was unobtainable. After a brief lifting of restrictions in the summer with buses on the boulevards and opera being resumed (evening dress prohibited) shops would not be lit after 6pm except where food and drink were sold and barbers' shops and pharmacies. Restaurants were to close thirty minutes earlier at 9.30 pm and places of entertainment had to close one night a week and cut their lighting by fifty per cent.

Germany was already experiencing real shortages that 'hit the industrial areas particularly hard, to the extent that production began to suffer'. Bread, rationed in February 1915, was now joined by meat, potatoes, milk, sugar, butter and soap. Fruit and vegetables along with game and poultry remained exempt but were not always easy to come by, and the latter were not always affordable. The situation was made worse by a poor harvest. As a result there was civil unrest with mobs demanding food. Naturally, there were no shortages for the rich and the black market thrived.

Germany also had shortages of textiles and other materials. Cotton was unobtainable and wool a luxury. Clothing now had to be darned, turned and patched to prolong its life. Even the production of ersatz fibres did little to help: nettle and willow fibres substituted for cotton.

In Germany, War Bread had been produced very soon after the start of the war and by 1916 all kinds of unpalatable and improbable food substitutes were being used. Coffee was made from a mixture of acorns, chicory, herbs and berries or roasted barley, milk was dried and powdered, various dried leaves were used as tea, and blood sausage replaced the preferred variety. Cake was made from chestnut flour and clover meal, and meat was made from vegetables. There were rice lamb chops, nut cutlets and vegetable beefsteak – 'a pale green concoction of cornmeal, spinach, potatoes and ground nuts bound with egg'. The list grew as the war lengthened.

Percentage food price increases in Britain from July 1914 to September 1916

Type of food	Percentage increase
Sugar	166
Fish	over 100
Eggs	over 100
Flour	66
Bread	58
Potatoes	53
Butter	54.5
Cheese	52
Bacon	49
Tea	50
Milk	39
Margarine	19

Price rises were accompanied by increases in taxation. The top rate of 6 per cent, established in Lloyd George's 'People's Budget' of 1909, had risen to 12.5 per cent in the autumn of 1914, to 17.5 per cent in 1915 and now stood at 25 per cent. The supertax rate was also increased.

However, there was no shortage of luxuries and for the better off there were still large joints of meat available, along with geese and turkeys at Christmas. While some were spending their newly found prosperity on furs and cheap jewellery, in general the consensus was that there was little to celebrate and that almost everyone looked sad and depressed. At church services across the land many of the congregation were dressed in mourning. The government's only concession to Christmas was to waive a recent restriction in order to allow people to have a bigger meal for Christmas lunch. One diarist recorded that 'to wish each other "Merry Christmas" is a mockery' and at a Christmas party given by the American Embassy in Berlin, when one poor child got up and asked for peace, everyone wept. The weather in London summed it all up – dank and foggy. No one would mourn the end of 1916.

Section 1
Recruiting and Departure

GWHF16_002. A group of four photos showing the call-up process for the early groups of Derby men. It was a relatively simple process as they had already attested and merely needed to exchange their khaki armlet for a uniform. These men had been called to the colours by a proclamation in the middle of December 1915 and given a month to make suitable arrangements for their departure. Groups 2, 3, 4, and 5 (single men aged 19 to 22) were to present themselves in batches on successive days, to prevent congestion at the recruiting stations. Photo 1 shows London recruits reporting at Whitehall; number 2 is a party entering at the White City recruiting station. In the third picture men are seen selecting their regiments and in the final photograph the men are shown handing in their armlets.

GWHF16_001. At the end of 1915 men had rushed to join the colours as Derby men (groups 1 to 46), volunteers with some choice as to their unit of service. Further manpower was added by the passing of the Military Service Act on 4 January 1916 which introduced conscription with men grouped by age. This meant that every British male resident in Britain but not Ireland was now eligible for service with single men being taken first in specified call-up groups/classes. The first single men were called up on 25 January. In this picture a Derby man, wearing his armlet, is reading the proclamation, posted in London, calling up the first four Derby groups.

GWHF16_003. When called up, conscripts were examined, attested and then marched to their barracks. This is a group of married conscripts after their examination, one of whom appears to be taking his wife and child with him.

GWHF16_004. Many local shops were owned by a single proprietor who, on call-up, either found someone to look after their business or simply closed it for the duration. This shows Mr Albert Vaughan, a tailor in Crowthorne, Berkshire, who was called up with Group 5 in mid-January. Ignoring official advice to dispose of his shop he placed a notice in his shop window announcing it would be 'Reopening after Victory'.

GWHF16_005. On attestation, each Derby recruit was technically in the army for one day and then became a reserve awaiting his call-up. A day's pay was a shilling and a day's billeting money was one shilling and ninepence so each was given two shillings and ninepence. These coins were given to a Derby recruit who decided to keep them.

GWHF16_006. The call-ups produced a considerable number of men in a day. Here is one day's recruits ready to march to the station.

CLASSIFICATION CERTIFICATE. Army Form W. 3

THIS IS TO CERTIFY that Mr. *C. F. Thompson*

residing at *71 Dorold Rd. Suptonstone*

was medically examined on *12 MAY 1916*

and classified as fit for :—

*1. General Service.
2. Field Service at Home.
3. Garrison Service :
   (a) Abroad.
   (b) At home.
4. Labour :
   (a) Abroad. *at home*
   (b) At home. *abroad*
5. Sedentary work, clerks, etc.
6. Totally unfit for any category of Military Service.
7. Rejected

It should be noted that if classified in (3) or (5) you will receiv least two months' notice before you are again called up for service.

12 MAY 1916 Date. *C E Bell* Signat

*Categories not applicable to be struck out. Stratford, LONDON, E. Stat

W. 307—7500 300,000(40) 4/16 H W V(P 282) Forms/W.3291/1

GWHF16_007. On call-up conscripts were examined and classified as their suitability for military service. Category 1 General Service meant that C. Thompson was almost certainly going to serve abroad in a comb area. Whether he survived is not known.

GWHF16_008. After being examined, recruits took the oath of allegiance before a magistrate.

GWHF16_009. Unlike early Kitchener recruits, Derby men were quickly kitted out, armed and billeted in army barracks. Here Viscount French of Ypres, commander of Home Forces, is watching Derby men at bayonet practice.

GWHF16_010. Older, married men, from Group 36 upwards, were given free instruction in munition making so they could be substituted for single men engaged in this work. The photo shows married men signing on for munition training.

GWHF16_011. Not every Derby recruit was able to go when called so tribunals heard their appeals for postponement to a later group. This was often due to family problems or the difficulty of finding suitable staff for their business to continue while they were away.

GWHF16_012. Not everyone wanted to fight. For a whole range of reasons there were men opposed to the war. Some would join but not fight, some would perform work of national importance but not join the military, while others would do neither. These conscientious objectors are employed on the construction of a military road in East Anglia.

GWHF16_013. Quakers were opposed to fighting but were prepared to serve their country in non-combatant ways. This group of Quakers are serving in the Red Cross and were photographed just before they left for France where they were to become the staff of a Quaker ambulance train.

GWHF16_014. The authorities in Britain had hoped that the Military Service Act would produce hundreds of thousands of new recruits. Instead the net increase was a mere 43,000 because 748,587 exemptions were granted on top of the 1,433,827 who were already in reserved occupations or wore an official war work badge. Fortunately there were other reserves of manpower available. When Germany declared war on Portugal in March 1916 it immediately mobilised and sent men to fight in Africa and within a year was providing a fighting presence on the Western Front.

GWHF16_015. Like Britain, Portugal became a military camp. Here Portuguese infantry are learning to shoulder arms.

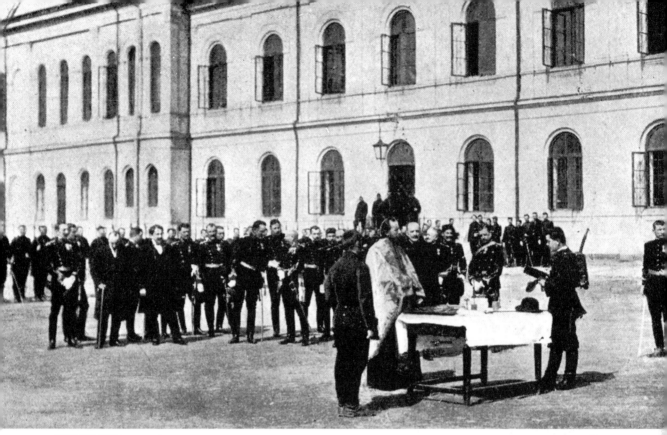

GWHF16_016. Five months after the Portuguese joined the Allied forces, an ill-prepared Romania declared war on Austria-Hungary. Here Romanian recruits are taking the oath after enlisting.

GWHF16_017. Romanian infantry on the frontier prior to launching attacks through the Carpathians and into Transylvania.

Section 2
Armament production and Home Defence

GWHF16_018. With both sides employing aggressive bombing campaigns, cities like London and Paris were brightly lit at night. This shows the searchlights in London captioned 'The Lights of London'.

GWHF16_019. Another photo of London showing the Thames Embankment when a Zeppelin raid was expected. The glare is the result of a long exposure photograph.

GWHF16_020. As the war progressed, London's defences improved. These are anti-aircraft guns in action during a raid. They sometimes did more damage than the raiders themselves when their shells fell in built-up areas.

GWHF16_021. As in London, defences around Paris increased during the war. This is an anti-aircraft machine gun on a rotating pedestal which was probably completely ineffective given the height that raiders flew.

GWHF16_022. Microphone listening posts were set up in London and Paris to detect approaching raiders. They magnified sounds and it was claimed that no aircraft could approach unheard.

GWHF16_023. Invasion was a constant threat and large numbers of troops were deployed to be prepared for such an occurrence. As more and more were needed at the front, only those in training could be spared for Home Defence, plus volunteer units made of men too young, too old or unfit for service. Some units accepted women. Here the Motor Volunteers in London, including women, are being inspected by the commanding officer of the London District, General Sir Francis Lloyd.

GWHF16_024. Women volunteers standing at attention during an inspection of the Motor Volunteers by Sir Francis Lloyd.

GWHF16_025. The importance of the machine gun was quickly realised and large orders were placed to bring battalions up to the required strength. A special training camp was set up at Belton Park near Grantham to provide personnel. These are motor machine gunners in training in the country lanes of England. Note the large amount of ammunition carried in the trailer.

GWHF16_026. It was quickly realised that cavalry, unless there was a breakthrough, were surplus men. As a result they regularly shared the trenches with the infantry. This meant that they had to be trained as infantry as well as cavalry. Here Royal Horse Guards are learning how to fortify a trench on a golf course near London.

GWHF16_027. Neutral countries also had to defend their territories. Here Swiss soldiers patrol the frontier.

GWHF16_028. As no one was likely to shoot at them, Swiss guards could walk around fully exposed in their lines and set up mobile searchlights to shine in to France or Germany to see what was happening in the opposing trenches.

GWHF16_029. One of the voluntary functions of the London National Guard was to accompany attested men on route marches.

GWHF16_030. Men of the City of London National Guard being sworn in by the Lord Mayor at the Guildhall.

GWHF16_031. On Saturday, 4 November, the Lord Mayor, Sir Charles Wakefield, opened the new headquarters of the City of London Territorial Association. Here the Lord Mayor is taking the salute at the march past of the 2nd Battalion of the City of London Volunteer Regiment.

GWHF16_032. Many older Derby men were trained in munition work to replace younger men. Special classes were set up to train them, with many women joining the classes before working in munitions factories. The illustration shows a Derby group class in the Shoreditch Technical Institute lecture hall.

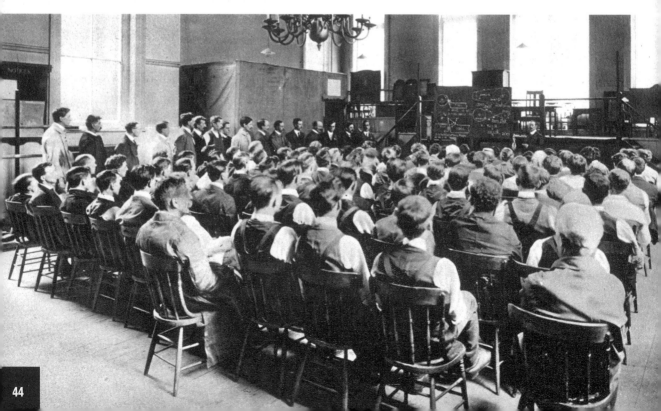

GWHF16_033. To help release men for the front, the French brought over thousands of men from its colonies to work in fields and factories. Here a volunteer from Indo-China is working on a lathe in a munitions factory.

GWHF16_036. Munitionettes assembling shell fuses in a British munitions factory.

GWHF16_034. As the front needed more and more munitions, the number of armament factories increased. These needed labour and with men at a premium their place was taken by women. An all-female munitions canteen at a large factory in Britain.

GWHF16_037. Manufacturing rifle cartridges for .303 rifles and machine guns.

GWHF16_035. All the belligerent countries suffered the same shortage – men. Canadian women war-workers in a munitions factory making time rings for shrapnel fuses. In this factory women did all the work except the heavy lifting and final packing for transport.

GWHF16_038. Women operating lathes in a munitions plant where even the inspectors are women.

GWHF16_039. An orderly queue to receive their dinner ticket in a munition factory.

GWHF16_041. A stall, complete with shells, set up for the Women's War Procession to encourage women to become munitions workers.

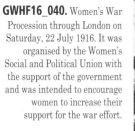

GWHF16_040. Women's War Procession through London on Saturday, 22 July 1916. It was organised by the Women's Social and Political Union with the support of the government and was intended to encourage women to increase their support for the war effort.

GWHF16_042. An all-male munitions canteen controlled by female charge-hands.

GWHF16_043. A factory dining hall at a munitions plant in Lyon with accommodation for 2,300 workers. More rustic in nature than its English counterparts it is adequately supplied with wine.

GWHF16_044. A Fren[ch] munitions factory with newly cast shells awaitir[g] filling.

GWHF16_046. A Fren[ch] skilled worker turning t[he] surface of a torpedo so it [is] smooth to reduce frictior[n] and reduce the possibilit[y of] early detonation.

GWHF16_045. Most contemporary images show army munitions being manufactured but all combatants had a navy that needed its own special supplies. Here French workers prepare a torpedo.

GWHF16_047. French 75mm field guns ready for despatch to the arsenal for checking prior to being sent to artillery parks near the front.

GWHF16_048. King George travelled a considerable distance during the war to visit his people at home and at the front. Here he is seen visiting the Birmingham Small Arms factory at Small Heath, Birmingham.

GWHF16_049. Munitions work was often dangerous and accidents happened regularly, some more serious than others. This picture shows some of the mass burial that resulted from the explosion of the explosives factory at Faversham, the worst in the history of the British explosives industry. At 2.20 pm on Sunday, 2 April, an explosion ripped through the gunpowder mill at Uplees, near Faversham, when a store of 200 tons of TNT was detonated after some empty sacks caught fire. The TNT and ammonium nitrate used to 'stretch' the TNT had exploded. The explosion was heard across the Thames estuary and as far away as Norwich and Great Yarmouth. In Southend-on-Sea domestic windows and two large plate-glass shop windows were broken. There were 115 deaths in the explosion and subsequent sympathetic detonations. All were men and boys, including all the Works Fire Brigade; no women were killed because they did not work on a Sunday. The bodies of seven victims were never found. 108 corpses were buried in this mass grave at Faversham Cemetery on 6 April.

GWHF16_050. There had been troubles in Ireland for many years prior to the war and when both loyalists and republicans had joined to fight the common enemy many felt there would be a respite, but in 1916 tensions came to a head resulting in the Easter Uprising. The Germans sent arms to the nationalists on the SMS *Aud*, actually SMS Libau, previously SS Castro. The ship had been built in Hull in 1907.

GWHF16_051. Newly armed Sinn Feiners marching through the streets on St Patrick's Day 1916.

GWHF16_053. A view of Eden Quay after the uprising.

GWHF16_052. Sir Roger Casement, an Anglo-Irish diplomat for the United Kingdom, humanitarian activist, Irish nationalist and poet. He was knighted for his human rights investigations in 1911 and was described as the 'father of twentieth century human rights investigations'. His fame turned to infamy for his efforts to gain German collaboration for an armed uprising in Ireland in 1916 to gain its independence. He was hanged at Pentonville Prison in London on 3 August 1916, at the age of 51.

GWHF16_054. Dublin ruins after the uprising had been suppressed.

GWHF16_055. The ruins of Liberty Hall after it had been captured by British soldiers.

GWHF16_056. While Republican snipers were still active it was dangerous for British soldiers to move about. A safe method of transport was the armoured boiler on wheels with cut-out gun ports.

GWHF16_057. British soldiers waiting to move on but pinned down by sniper fire on the Kingstown Road at Ballsbridge.

GWHF16_058. British soldiers guarding the Great Northern main line in Dublin in the north-east of the city.

GWHF16_059. A barricade in Townsend Street.

GWHF16_060. With the fighting over the rebels were marched off to barracks.

GWHF16_062. Some of the Sinn Feiners who were kept at Richmond barracks in Dublin.

GWHF16_061. Within less than a week the uprising was over and several hundred rebels were taken into captivity, some of whom were transported to England where they were imprisoned.

GWHF16_063. A number of the rebels were executed for their part in the rebellion. Sean MacDermott was one of the signatories of the rebellion manifesto who was shot on 12 May 1916.

GWHF16_064. The rebel Commander-in-Chief and President of the Provisional Government, Padraig Pearse, was also shot for his part in the uprising.

GWHF16_065. James Connolly, Commandant-General of the Dublin Division, was executed on 12 May.

GWHF16_066. The trial of Roger Casement drew full galleries at the Old Bailey.

Section 3
Raids and U-boats

GWHF16_067. On 3 September 1916 the German airship SL11 was shot down by Lieutenant Leefe Robinson and crashed in Cuffley during an aerial bombardment intended for London. He was awarded the Victoria Cross. A major tourist draw, the military took the wreckage away for examination, recycling and selling parts to raise funds for the war effort. Here RFC men are loading a propeller from the airship.

GWHF16_068. Skeleton of the L33 brought down on 24 September. It was damaged by anti-aircraft fire and forced to land at New Hall Farm, Little Wigborough, twenty yards from a nearby house. As the airship hit the ground the occupants of the house, a man, his wife and three children, ran for their lives, followed by the airship's crew. Shortly afterwards the commander, Kapitan Bocker, set fire to it. Special Constable Edgar Nicholas, who lived nearby, made his way to the scene and came across a group of men walking along the road who identified themselves as the Zeppelin crew. He arrested them although they were armed. Other officers later joined them and the local constable, PC Charles Smith, arranged for the prisoners to be handed over to the military to be taken off to a prisoner-of-war camp.

GWHF16_070. The gondolas and propellers of the L33 destroyed in South Essex.

GWHF16_069. Earlier in the year the L15 had sunk off the Kent coast. The commander of the airship was Kapitanleutnant Joachim Breithaupt. On 31 March 1916 at 21.45 hours, it received a direct hit from the AA gun at Purfleet, Essex. The AA shell damaged four of the gas cells (numbers 9, 11, 12, and 16) and the L15 began to lose height, despite the crew throwing everything out in an attempt to lose weight. As the L15 got closer to earth, it was attacked by 2nd Lieutenant Alfred de Bathe Brandon RFC, who climbed above the airship and tried to destroy it by dropping incendiary bombs and Ranken darts onto the top of the hull. This was not successful. Eventually the Zeppelin came down in the sea off Margate at 00.15 (1 April) close to the Kentish Knock lightship. One of the seventeen-man crew was drowned; the rest were rescued by the armed trawler *Olivine* and later transferred to the destroyer HMS *Vulture*.

GWHF16_071. Lord French, commander of Home Forces, inspecting the L32, shot down on 24 September. It had received hits from anti-aircraft fire and was attacked by 2nd Lieutenant Sowrey with incendiary ammunition.

GWHF16_072. The Zeppelin L77 was shot down near Revigny on 21 February 1916 by motor anti-aircraft fire. The airship exploded when it hit the ground killing all the crew who, according to the original caption, were found dead in the gondola pictured.

GWHF16_073. A military funeral was accorded the crew of the SL11, shot down on 3 September by Leefe Robinson.

GWHF16_075. Kapitanleutnant Joachim Breithaupt, commander of the L15.

GWHF16_074. A Warrant Officer of the L15 captured off Margate. Before the war he had worked on a steamer trading between Hamburg and the East Coast.

GWHF16_076. Lieutenant Brandon had dropped bombs on the descending airship L15 after it had been hit by anti-aircraft fire.

GWHF16_078. The German Navy attacked Britain with airships, submarines and capital ships. Throughout the war there were fire and flee operations along the east coast, starting in December 1914. This is a faulty shell, under guard, from one of the German ships that bombarded the town. Numerous residences were damaged by the shelling.

GWHF16_079. A house in Lowestoft clearly showing damage from the shelling on 25 April.

GWHF16_082. Typical of the damage caused by a direct hit. The bomb destroyed the house and damaged neighbouring properties. In the centre house a woman, girl and boy were killed and in the other houses several persons were injured.

GWHF16_081. A shop in Paris damaged by a Zeppelin bomb.

GWHF16_080. Shell-shattered business premises on a main street in Lowestoft.

GWHF16_083. This Lowestoft house was hit by a naval shell which also injured a special constable and two women.

GWHF16_084. On 29 January LZ49 attacked Paris and dropped 18 bombs on the city, killing 26 and injuring 32. Those killed were given a national funeral.

GWHF16_085. One bomb from the airship LZ49 caused a large hole in the roof of the Metro.

GWHF16_088. In January, German airships dropped bombs on Paris on two consecutive nights. This is a house damaged on the first night. The second raid caused little damage but Parisians demanded reprisals.

GWHF16_086. A large residence on the Lowestoft sea front reduced to ruins by German shells.

GWHF16_087. A mission hall in Burton-on-Trent was wrecked by a bomb, which struck the ground a few yards in front of the building. A lady who was addressing the meeting and three members of the congregation were killed.

GWHF16_089. A five-storey house in Paris completely wrecked by a bomb from a Zeppelin dropped during the first of two consecutive raids on 29 and 30 January.

GWHF16_090. Although neutral, America supplied Britain with considerable amounts of munitions and so was a target for German espionage. Here firemen are cooling down the remains of a munitions depot on Black Tom Island in New Jersey. A series of small fires, caused by German agents, caused a kiloton of ammunition and TNT to explode causing considerable damage to the area around the depot. The explosion was felt as far away as Philadelphia and was comparable to an earthquake measuring between 5 and 5.5 on the Richter scale.

GWHF16_092. The Canadian Parliament buildings in Ottawa caught fire on 3 February. Initially it was believed to the work of enemy saboteurs but a Royal Commission concluded that the cause was accidental.

GWHF16_091. Another view of the Black Tom explosion that occurred between 2 and 3 am on 30 July.

Section 4
Propaganda

GWHF16_093. There was considerable propaganda value in widely reporting British success both for the Home Front and neutral countries. Heroes were always welcome and Leefe Robinson VC was the man of the hour when he brought down a Zeppelin over Cuffley.

GWHF16_094. Earlier in the year Flight-Commander Bone had been the man of the moment for his work in home defence.

GWHF16_095. While most metal from crashed Zeppelins was melted down for reuse, souvenirs like this ash tray were not only of propaganda value but were worth more financially than the metal they were made of. This was sold to raise funds for the Red Cross.

GWHF16_096. A machine gun from a downed Zeppelin photographed for the newspapers and later used for a propaganda display in London.

GWHF16_098. Special Constable Ed Nicholas, the man wh arrested the crew of L33.

GWHF16_097. While most of this wire from a crashed Zeppelin would be melted down, small lengths were sold to raise money for war charities.

GWHF16_099. Captured war material was displayed by both sides to show how well they were doing. This is a photograph of such an exhibition held at Finsbury Park. The observation car hanging above the visitors was, according to the original caption, jettisoned or lost over East Anglia during the course of an air raid, along with hundreds of yards of connecting wire.

GWHF16_100. The procession of the Lord Mayor of London's show was a good place to exhibit captured war booty.

GWHF16_101. Les Invalides was used by the French government to display captured German war trophies, an idea which the British copied.

GWHF16_102. *UC-5* ran aground while on patrol 27 April 1916 and was scuttled. Her crew were captured by HMS *Firedrake* and the submarine was displayed at Temple Pier on the Thames river and, later, in Central Park in New York for propaganda purposes.

GWHF16_103. A captured 'Albrecht' mortar on display in a park. These were made of wood and bound with iron and came in several calibres. They fired a projectile called a coal bucket.

GWHF16_104. Civilian bravery, especially where British soldiers were involved, was very good propaganda. This is Mademoiselle Émilienne Moreau (right in picture), who was known as the Heroine of Loos, on the sands at Trouville with her mother. A few weeks prior she had been awarded the British Military Medal and the Order of St John of Jerusalem by the British Ambassador in Paris. 'A girl of seventeen, during the battle of Loos she saw some Germans firing on the British from a cellar. She courageously went to the rescue, and shot two of the enemy with a revolver, killing three more with hand-grenades.'

GWHF16_105. In June the King received a party of Russian PoWs who had escaped from the Germans, and inspected them in Buckingham Palace grounds.

GWHF16_106. The annual 14 July celebration continued even though there was a war going on. Included in the procession for 1916 were Allied troops. This is the Russian contingent who were probably very pleased to be in France.

GWHF16_107. Propaganda was used to motivate. This is one the footballs kicked by men of the 8th East Surrey Regiment as they charged German positions at Carnoy. They successfully took the positions and the balls were recovered after the battle and used as a symbol of heroism. Here the commanding officer of the East Surreys' depot is showing it to new recruits.

GWHF16_108. Flags are important symbols: rallying points, signs of determination. On 1 July the flags of HMS *Kent* were taken in procession to Canterbury Cathedral for permanent display as a sign of the bravery shown by the men of the ship. The flags, presented to the ship by the ladies of Kent, were badly damaged during the battle at the Falklands Islands in December 1914. The pieces were picked up by Captain Allen and restored by the Ladies' Committee of the Association of the Men of Kent and Kentish Men.

GWHF16_109. One way of showing how patriotic you were and also providing a good piece of propaganda was giving large amounts of money. This aircraft was a war gift from residents in the Punjab. It is pictured as it is about to leave for front-line service in France.

GWHF16_113. A high profile hero was Captain Charles Fryatt of the SS *Brussels*. He was executed by the Germans for attempting to ram a U-boat in 1915. When his ship was captured off the Netherlands in 1916, he was court-martialled and sentenced to death although he was a civilian non-combatant. As with the execution of Nurse Cavell, international outrage followed his execution near Bruges in Belgium. In 1919 his body was reburied in Dovercourt in the United Kingdom, with full honours.

GWHF16_112. Pictured on 16 November, outside Buckingham Palace, is Mr William Williams, who is wearing his son's Victoria Cross. It had been won by Able Seaman William Charles Williams, during the landing of men on Gallipoli from the *River Clyde*.

GWHF16_111. Medals awarded posthumously or to men who had died after their act of bravery were received by their relatives. These are the parents of Private Edward Butler of the Grenadier Guards who was killed leading a grenade attack. They are pictured shortly after the investiture.

GWHF16_110. Nurses leaving Buckingham Palace after being awarded the Royal Red Cross of the Second Class for services in France.

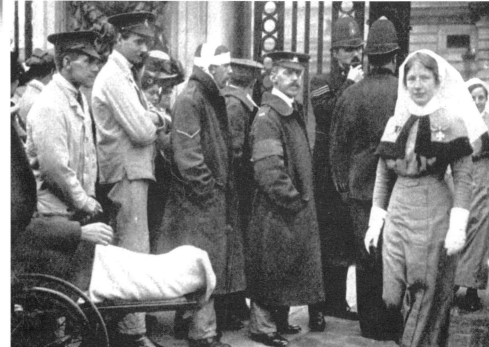

Section 5
Prisoners and Occupation

GWHF16_115. With a shortage of British men, PoWs were put to work in a large range of capacities to replace them.

GWHF16_114. A parade of PoWs on their arrival in England was good for civilian morale and a sign that the war was going well.

GWHF16_116. Stories of escaped PoWs were infrequent but good for morale. French aviator Eugène Gilbert had bombed the Zeppelin building sheds by Lake Constance the previous year. Mechanical problems forced him to land in Switzerland where he was interned. He successfully escaped on the third attempt.

GWHF16_117. Many repatriated soldiers went through Switzerland, so many that the postal authorities had to organise a special department to deal with it. Most of the parcels shown in this photo had been redirected from German prison camps.

GWHF16_119/119a. Two photos taken during a half-hour halt in Zurich station for British PoWs from Germany who were being exchanged. Their new place of internment was Château d'Oex near Montreux.

GWHF16_118. Wives and relatives of wounded British prisoners in Switzerland starting from London Waterloo to visit them. The parties were organised and taken out under the auspices and through the instrumentality of the Lord Kitchener Memorial Fund, and travel was in charge of the Red Cross.

GWHF16_120. This was the German Swiss Commission before which the British prisoners about to be exchanged were brought for a second and final examination. The standing figure marked with an X is Prince Max of Baden.

GWHF16_121. On 6 September 1914, as they were advancing on Senlis, shots were fired at the German troops. In revenge they shot the Mayor and five other hostages. For whatever reason, they allowed a memorial service a year later for the victims.

GWHF16_122. A student procession at Warsaw on the German declaration of the Kingdom of Poland. This was an attempt to legitimise their occupation and show the Polish population that they were there to liberate Poland from Russia.

Section 6
Casualties

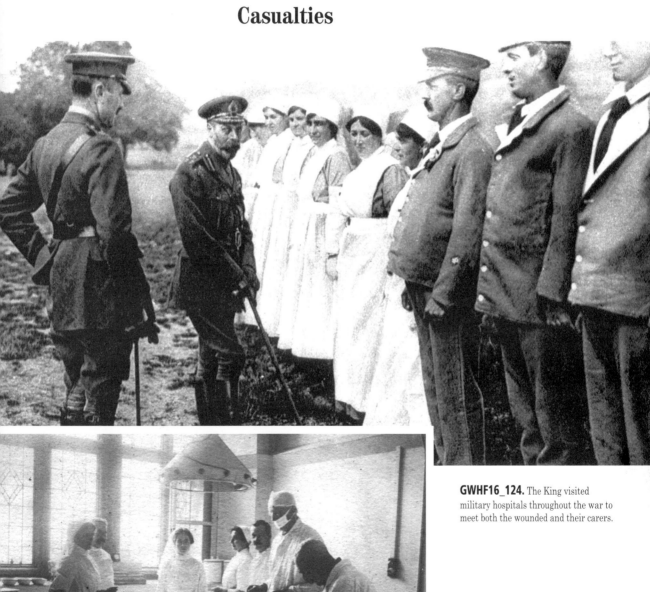

GWHF16_124. The King visited military hospitals throughout the war to meet both the wounded and their carers.

GWHF16_123. A hospital well behind the lines with male and female medical personnel.

GWHF16_126. This is a factory in Germany making prosthetic legs, similar to those manufactured in England that would be worn by the soldier in the opposite photograph.

GWHF16_127. Making wooden legs for German soldiers.

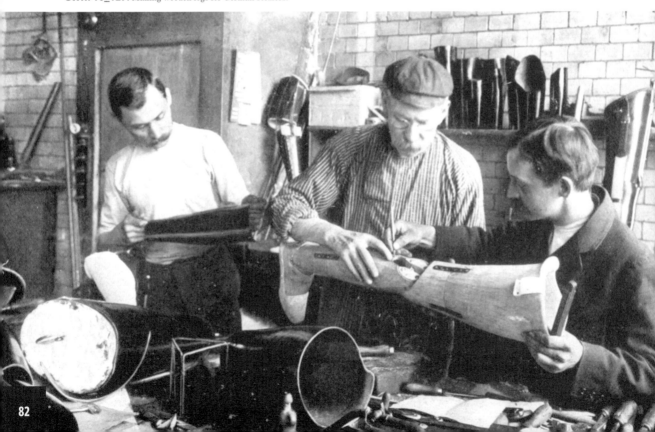

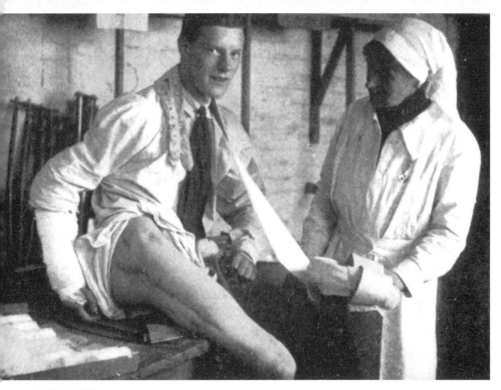

GWHF16_125. Depending on their point of view many would have seen a wound like this as a blessing. Here the nurse is making a stump bucket with a plaster bandage.

GWHF16_128. Once fitted, the new owners had to be trained in how to use them. This group of German soldiers are being taught agricultural skills.

GWHF16_129. Men on the roof of a hospital somewhere in England recuperating from wounds received during the Somme battles.

GWHF16_130. Whenever possible the wounded were provided with difficult-to-come-by foodstuffs like eggs and treated to excursions when the weather permitted. This is the MV *Britannia*, a pleasure cruiser on the Thames that carried men from the Reading area up and down the Thames.

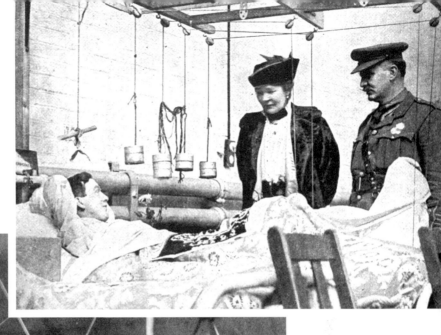

GWHF16_131. Mrs Astor opened a hospital for wounded Canadians near Taplow. This is the Duchess of Connaught on her return from Canada in 1916, visiting Canadians under treatment there.

GWHF16_132. When the exchanged PoWs arrived in Britain they were still convalescent. Here some of the newly released men are talking to a fellow exchange before his ascent.

GWHF16_136. Municipal consideration for wounded soldiers: a seat for their special benefit in Harrow. These were placed in the streets around the town and each was inscribed, 'For the use of Wounded soldiers'.

GWHF16_135. (Above right) Wherever there were war hospitals there was generally a war hospital supply depot. All work was voluntary and all materials provided by funds from collections, sales, auctions or donations. This is the depot at Belgravia.

GWHF16_133. The Tsar's Winter Palac doubled as a Red Cross hospital and in the entrance hall as a factory: the girls are making respirators.

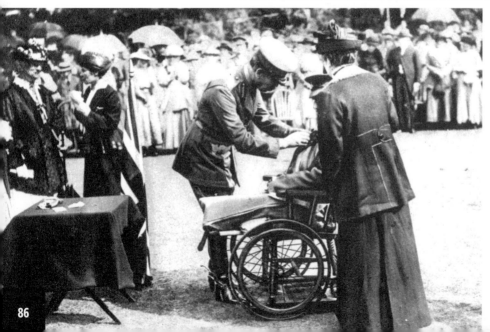

GWHF16_134. This photograph was take at the newly opened Queen Mary's Worksh at the military hospital, Brighton Pavilion. workshop had been founded by Queen Mary train disabled soldiers in various skilled industries – electrical engineering, carpent typewriting among others. Major General S Francis Lloyd, on behalf of the King, is seen here presenting the DCM to Sergeant Grim for bravery at Armentières in 1914 where h lost both legs.

GWHF16_138. As in Britain, German towns constructed memorials to their dead. This memorial is at Bärringen (Pernink in the Czech Republic). Over the coat of arms is a small shield inscribed Kriegsjahr (war year) 1914-1915.

GWHF16_139. The roll of honour at Palace Road, Hackney. From this street more than 100 men voluntarily enlisted and those at the front were recorded on the roll.

GWHF16_140. On 4 August, the Lord Mayor, Colonel Sir Charles Wakefield (seated on the right), unveiled this Gothic cross in the churchyard of St Botolph's, Bishopsgate. The cross was in memory of Lord Kitchener, Jack Cornwell, boy hero of Jutland and of the fallen officers and men of the Honourable Artillery Company.

GWHF16_141. Individual memorials were placed in appropriate places to remember the fallen. This wreath was placed over the seat formerly occupied by Mr Kenneth Hallward of the Worcestershire Regiment, who was killed in action. Before joining the army he was in the choir at St Michael's, Bedford Park.

GWHF16_143. A war monument at Friedrichshafen to Field Marshal von Hindenburg.

GWHF16_142. A Gotha *Taube* was set up to the memory of airmen killed in the war in the town of Gotha.

GWHF16_145. Fallen airmen of both sides were generally given an appropriate funeral. This is the funeral of Captain Schramm, commander of the airship shot down at Cuffley.

GWHF16_144. A French escort of honour of infantry head the procession of the funeral of a British airman who died of wounds received in a dogfight. Whenever possible, the French provided such a guard of honour.

GWHF16_146. The funeral procession of the naval boy hero, Jack Cornwell, is seen here leaving East Ham Town Hall.

GWHF16_147. The United States was neutral but had its own problems on the Mexican border. This is the funeral of an American officer killed fighting the Mexicans.

GWHF16_149. After his death in action, Captain Boelcke was laid out in state in St John's Church at Dessau.

GWHF16_148. The Emperor of Japan, on learning that Commander Shimomura of the Japanese Navy had perished at the Battle of Jutland, ordered a special funeral service to be held for him at the pavilion in Aoyama cemetery. The service was attended by Admiral Togo.

GWHF16_151. Only twelve survived the sinking of HMS *Hampshire*. The body of Lieutenant Colonel Fitzgerald, Kitchener's personal military secretary, was recovered from the sea and brought to London. His coffin was placed in All Souls Chapel of St Matthew's Church in Great Peter Street, Westminster.

GWHF16_150. This is the last photograph of Lord Kitchener while in London on 2 June to meet a group of MPs. After the meeting he went, with his staff, to the cruiser *Hampshire* for his journey to Russia.

Frommes Andenken im Gebete
an den tugendsamen

Jgl. Lorenz Reiter

Gütlerssohn v. Iglberg, Pf. Ranoldsberg
Soldat beim 16. Inf.-Regmt. 8. Komp.
welcher am 11 November 1916 in einem
Alter von 20 Jahren 4 Monaten den Helden-
tod fürs Vaterland starb.
Es ist nun das **zweite** Opfer fürs Vaterland.
Ach, zu früh bist du geschieden,
Umsonst war unser heißes Fleh'n.
Ruhe sanft in Gottes Frieden
Bis wir uns einstens wiederseh'n.
Mein Jesus Barmherzigkeit!   (100 Tage Abl.)

D. Geiger, Mühldorf

GWHF16_152. There was a Women's War Procession through London on Saturday, 22 July 1916, organised by the Women's Social and Political Union with the support of the government. The procession was intended to encourage women to increase their support for the war effort. The event included groups of women war workers dressed in their work clothes, including munitions workers.

GWHF16_155. Lorenz Deiter was killed on the Somme during the last big British attacks, fighting with 16 Infantry Regiment.

GWHF16_153. (Left) Many of the dead were commemorated at home. This is a mourning card for William Francis who died during the Jutland battle.

In Memory of

LEADING WIREMAN

WILLIAM THOMAS FRANCIS,

AGED 26 YEARS.

Who was lost on H.M.S. " Invincible,"
during the Naval Battle in the North Sea,
31st May, 1916.

GWHF16_154. A German mourning card for Ludwig Schnellenberger.

Ehre dem Andenken
des ehrengeachteten Herrn

Ludwig Schnellenberger

Taglöhner in Reut, Trainsoldat,
welcher am 3. März 1916 in Dou...
infolge eines Gehirnschlages i...
38. Lebensjahre den Heldentod für
Vaterland gestorben ist.

Frisch und gesund ging ich von der lb. Heimat fo...
Mein Leben mußte ich opfern im Feindes Ort;
Beim Abschied drückte ich euch noch die Hand
Dann ging ich u. kämpfte für Gott, König, Vaterlan...
Vergeßt mich nicht u. betet Herr verzeih uns. Sünd...
Dann werden wir uns im Himmel wieder finden.

Druck von A. Lehner, Simbach a. Inn.

HE HATH DONE WHAT HE COULD.

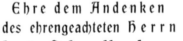

Zum frommen Andenken im Gebete
an den tugendsamen Jüngling

Josef Huber,

Bäcker, Oekonomenssohn v. Gangkofen,
Soldat beim 16. Inf.-Rgt., 6. Komp.,
welcher im Alter von 22 Jahren 5 Monaten am 3. Juli 1916 nachts schwer verwundet wurde und am 4. Juli in einem Feldlazarett bei Arras den Heldentod fürs Vaterland gestorben ist.

GWHF16_156. Like Lorenz Reiter, Josef Huber was also killed on the Somme, but in the first days of the British attack. They served in the same regiment.

IN AFFECTIONATE REMEMBRANCE OF

Corporal F. Taylor,

OF THE 6TH DUKE OF WELLINGTON'S REGIMENT.

KILLED IN FRANCE, AUGUST 29TH, 1916.

AGED 22 YEARS.

A loving nephew, a faithful friend,
One of the best that God could lend;
He nobly answered duty's call,
His life he gave for one and all,
But the unknown grave is the bitterest blow,
None but an aching heart can know.

From his loving Aunt and Uncle,   12, Elliott Street,
and Cousin.   Silsden.

GWHF16_158. Corporal Taylor's family remembered him with a photographic mourning card. He was 22 at the time of his death, serving with the 1st/6th West Riding Regiment, and is buried in Lonsdale Cemetery, Authuille.

In Remembrance

OF

PRIVATE,

George Dugdall Banning,

Who Died of Wounds
received in Action
in France,
July 4th, 1916.

Aged 22 Years.

Interred St. Severs Cemetery,
Rouen.

Not now but in the coming years,
It may be in the better land,
We'll read the meaning of our tears,
And there sometime we'll
understand.

270, St. Georges Road,
Hull.

GWHF16_157. The author's great-uncle died of shell wounds. His family commemorated his death with silk book marks which were given to friends and family members.

GWHF16_160. Queen Mary placing flowers on a roll of honour in South Hackney.

GWHF16_161. The memorial service at Westminster Abbey on 25 April was in honour of the ANZAC troops who fell in Gallipoli. Attending the service along with the King were 1,300 Australian and 700 New Zealand troops who were in England on sick leave.

GWHF16_162. On 6 June an Army order was issued that commanded officers to wear mourning with their uniforms for one week commencing 7 June 1916. This photograph shows officers when changing the guard at Buckingham Palace on 7 June. Each is wearing a black crêpe band on their left arm.

GWHF16_163. On 21 November, Emperor Franz Josef died at Schönbrunn Palace. He is seen here lying in state, in the uniform of a Field Marshal. His body was taken at night by torchlight escort to Hofburg Chapel.

GWHF16_164. Admiral Jellicoe is here bidding farewell to Lord Kitchener prior to him leaving for Russia on 5 June.

Section 7
Wartime life

GWHF16_166. While women tramcar and lorry drivers were a topic of debate in London, in Bordeaux, pictured, they were already running whole cars: a female driver and ticket collector in action.

GWHF16_165. With millions of men now serving with the colours, there were many more jobs now available to women. This is a London bus conductress ringing the bell.

GWHF16_167. It was the same in Germany: a shortage of men meant female employment in previously male domains. Here are two German railway workers, both female.

GWHF16_169. In 1916 the Post Office found that it needed to employ women as drivers. Here is one seen setting off on her round.

GWHF16_171. Ambulances continued to run throughout the war but after 1916 they were mainly driven and attended by women.

GWHF16_168. Not yet ready to employ women as drivers, the employers had little choice but to employ them as ticket collectors, porters and in most other capacities.

GWHF16_170. Another traditionally male area was that of chauffeur. As there were not enough males available women soon settled into the role. This is the chauffeur of the Duchess of Marlborough.

GWHF16_173. Female crane drivers showing off their feminine but practical and workmanlike clothing, coloured chocolate with blue piping.

GWHF16_172. The increase in working women needed a police force that 'fitted the bill'. By 1916 there were numerous female police officers on patrol. They were very much in demand at munitions factories where most of the employed were women.

GWHF16_174. (Left) This photo, taken in Chew Magna, shows either Mrs Summers or her daughter, making domestic gas – under the supervision of a male manager.

GWHF16_175. Clad in brown overalls, and looking somewhat French, these are two female window cleaners.

GWHF16_176. With millions serving in the armed forces, there were millions of parcels to sort and deliver. A sorting office staffed by women with a female supervisor.

GWHF16_177. Not all parcels could be delivered. Some men had died, some had moved unit or were in hospital. For the latter two categories it could be a while before the parcel caught up with them. In the case of the former, the parcel would be returned to the sender. Here women are attempting to return parcels that have been insufficiently addressed, e.g. Pte J Smith, London Regiment, BEF.

GWHF16_178. Possibly not the most fragrant of jobs but probably quite well paid. Here the women are seen cultivating bacteria on filter beds somewhere in the Midlands. They are dressed completely in rubber.

GWHF16_179. A war did not always stop investment in public transport. Here German women are digging an underground railway in Berlin. With few men available the women are doing the heavy work.

GWHF16_180. Female manual labour at Coventry gasworks loading coke into barrows. The coke was a by-product of coal gas production and was sold to consumers for domestic heating.

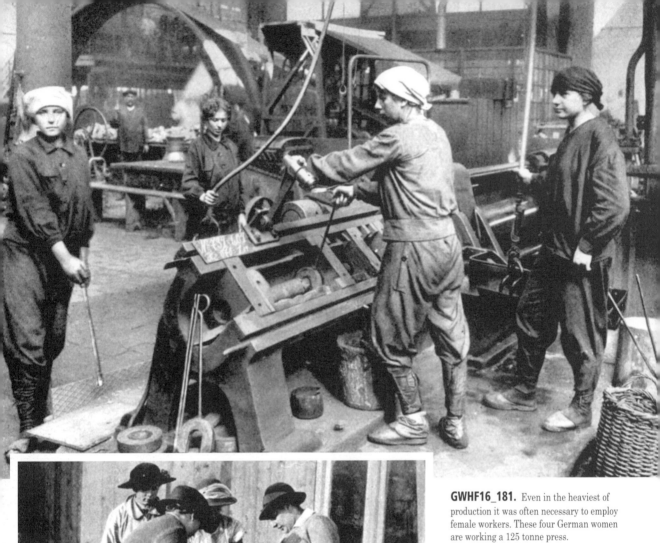

GWHF16_181. Even in the heaviest of production it was often necessary to employ female workers. These four German women are working a 125 tonne press.

GWHF16_183. Mr W. Tarrant, an Army hut contractor from Byfleet, was given permission to take a large number of women carpenters to France. At the time of the photograph he was training over thirty women, and behind them, although new to the work, are the walls and floors of seven portable huts, completed in just one day.

GWHF16_182. Ladies in a depot for convalescent remounts – sick or wounded horses being treated until fit for further service.

GWHF16_184. Well known in Irish sporting circles, Miss M.K. McVeagh was employed by Finchley Urban Council to water the roads.

GWHF16_185. The town council of Thetford appointed Miss Florrie Clark, who was only 15, to be town crier and official bill-poster in the absence of her father, who had joined the army. Here she is seen at work.

GWHF16_186. There was no longer any point in worrying about women doing heavy work as there were few men left to do it. Two soldiers' wives are seen here on Lord Onslow's Clandon estate sawing timber they had just felled.

GWHF16_189. Women were employed in the manufacture as well as the tuning of pianos during the war.

GWHF16_187. Here Miss Austin is shown taking the place of the normal van man in her father's bakery business. After completing her round she went to her home in Lenzie, near Glasgow, to help with the family poultry.

GWHF16_188. As some foodstuffs became scarce, people were told to grow their own. Open spaces across the country were put to use. This golf course at Sandy Hook, while still being used as it was intended and carefully maintained by female staff or boys, was also used as a poultry farm and for growing potatoes and other vegetables. The photograph shows a greens-woman and a girl mowing one of the greens.

GWHF16_191. The harvest, in this case grapes for wine, had to be brought in. Here, German women in the Rhine valley are seen picking the future 1916 vintage.

GWHF16_190. At Coombe Hill School, King's Langley, all the pupils were 'taught the art of domesticity'. Here some of the pupils are seen caring for the goats.

GWHF16_192. Even those who were financially more secure often made sure that there would be sufficient food by converting part of their grounds to animal husbandry. Here, Mrs Lowther, wife of the Speaker of the House of Commons, the Right Hon James Lowther PC MP is seen feeding the pigs at his house in Campsey Ashe, Suffolk.

GWHF16_193. Women involved in the French 1916 vintage are seen here handling the barrels to be used to mature the grape liquor.

GWHF16_194. Women replaced men across the land on farms. These are three members of the Women's Land Army working on a Royal Farm.

GWHF16_195. In 1916 the majority of ploughing was still done by horse but things were changing. A woman fieldworker demonstrating ploughing on an Oxfordshire farm.

GWHF16_196. Many farmers did not take kindly to women working the land but by late 1916 there was no choice. Here, at the Collingham Farmers' Club annual ploughing competition – which would normally have been an all-male preserve – spectators are watching two women work a tractor and four-furrow plough.

GWHF16_198. As horses became scarcer in Germany, any animal big enough was substituted. In the spring of 1916 this German farmer's wife is using two of their dairy cows to prepare the ground for planting.

GWHF16_197. The term munitions, in its broadest sense, covers everything required for military equipment. This is the interior of a depot for collecting and despatching shirts manufactured from workshops across France. The size of the mountain of shirts gives an idea of the number of men at the front.

GWHF16_199. With some foodstuffs scarce, classes were held to enable families still to eat well with the foods available. The Food Controller issued a voluntary edict to help reduce demand for foods like meat. Here the Mayor of Keighley is speaking to a group of boys about the need to eat less – hardly what growing boys wanted to think about.

GWHF16_200. The wartime equivalent of today's 'reduced' section in supermarkets but with no sell-by date involved. In order to provide for French soldiers' wives, every day-trader at the French equivalent of Covent Garden sold the previous days' vegetables at reduced prices.

GWHF16_201. By late 1916 the queue had become part of shopping. Whenever word got out that one retailer had supplies of a needed grocery, a queue would form, often big enough to warrant a policeman to maintain it in an orderly fashion. This queue was in North London, for potatoes.

GWHF16_202. A Glasgow
queue.

GWHF16_204. In Britain, boy
scouts collected conkers for
military use – glycerine
extraction. In Germany cherry
stones were also collected for the
same reason. This is a weighing
station for cherry pits.

GWHF16_203. The Germans
were quicker to provide mass
eating facilities as a way of
controlling food consumption.
The people in this queue in
Charlottenburg, a Berlin suburb,
are having their cards stamped
in order to buy their family meal.

GWHF16_205. Rabbit has always been a food that some like and some don't and was often eaten by the poorest in society. With decreasing supplies of beef, mutton and pork Germany, eating rabbit became a necessity. This is a rabbit farm in Hanover, where before the war rabbits were classe as vermin. In 1916 they were a desirable piece of meat.

GWHF16_207. Open spaces across Britain became allotments if the local council allowed. Here a family is working on an allotment in suburban parkland.

GWHF16_206. In London, empty spaces were often used for temporary huts to house transient military personnel. They were also used to grow extra food. The site of an old building in Kensington is here being employed in both capacities.

GWHF16_208. The railways allowed employees to cultivate the embankments, even though it was potentially dangerous.

GWHF16_209. Members of the Women's Volunteer Reserve are seen here cultivating waste land in Finchley. When ready it was planted with vegetables.

GWHF16_210. The food shortage was even more acute in Germany than it was in Britain. Here German pork butchers are weighing stock in an inspector's presence.

GWHF16_211. In Berlin large-scale cookers like those used by the army were used to provide cheap, nutritious meals for the inhabitants. A 'Gulaschkanon' held 200 litres of food that sold at 35 pfennigs a litre.

GWHF16_213. Potatoes being peeled to go into the 'Gulaschkanon' with the cabbage. There was little meat added to these meals.

GWHF16_212. Making the food for the 'Gulaschkanon' took a lot of preparation. Here cabbages are being cut up for boiling.

GWHF16_214. A war cooker before leaving the depot for distribution of the midday meal.

GWHF16_215. Boys and girls were just as involved with war work as their parents. Many schools held extra classes after school to help the war effort. Children knitted, made bags, sacks and hospital equipment in large quantities, saving the government money in their endeavours.

GWHF16_216. Female aristocrats often had their own favourite fund or charity. Lady Byron collected and sent socks to members of the Tank Corps. She was based at Byron Cottage, Hampstead Heath.

GWHF16_217. Each branch of the services had its own civilian organisation prepared to try and look after its needs, not always patronised by the wealthy. These two ladies are packing jerseys and socks for the British and Foreign Sailors' Society.

GWHF16_220. Money was as essential as bullets for both sides. An easy and quick method of collecting it was a flag day. This is a collection for the Red Cross somewhere in Germany.

GWHF16_218. At the Arts and Crafts School, Chailey, Sussex, 100 crippled children (could we use this expression today?) made crutches, splints, tables and other requisites for use in military hospitals.

GWHF16_221. Many different ways of collecting were tried. Lady Sophie Scott, the Judge at the Southern Cairn terrier Club's first Championship show at Ranelagh, is seen here with Mrs Hunloke's Shetland pony 'Midge', collecting on behalf of the British Sportsmen's Ambulance Fund.

GWHF16_219. Much of the manufacture of glass bottles was done in Belgium. With a shortage of glass, medicine bottles became valuable. This Islington boy scout is collecting them to raise money to provide motor ambulances for the front.

GWHF16_223. The flag day was international. Taken in Gibraltar, this scene could have been just about anywhere in the British Empire. This 'Our Day' collection, on 20 January, was for the Red Cross and raised £3,000 in Gibraltar, and over £3,100 in Malta.

GWHF16_225. Honouring the graves of the men who saved Paris. On the second anniversary of the Battle of the Marne a woman is putting a contribution in a box inscribed, 'For the upkeep of the graves in the *arrondissement* at Meaux'.

GWHF16_226. Queen Alexandra with Jeannie Jackson in front of the ambulance she bought. The daughter of a Burnley miner, she collected £1,100 in coppers in twelve months, £450 of which was spent on this Young Kitchener Motor Ambulance.

GWHF16_224. Britons across the world joined in collecting money for the war effort. These children, Mrs Jarley's (Canon Gairdner) Waxworks, toured Cairo and its suburbs raising money for the Red Cross.

GWHF16_227. Animals were useful tools in collecting money. This dog is collecting for the German Red Cross.

GWHF16_228. On 6 and 7 June a 'War Fair' was held at the Caledonian Market to raise money for the wounded. There were various goods and services on offer, mostly from the very rich. Here Lady Markham is offering to sell 20,000 tons of coal for the wounded.

GWHF16_229. At the Caledonian Market Mrs Astor was selling antiques for the wounded.

GWHF16_231. The French Empire also collected money to help the war effort. This is the collecting booth on 'Poilus' Day' at Bondoukou, capital of the Ivory Coast.

GWHF16_233. Another German statue to knock nails into to raise money.

GWHF16_232. A more German way of collecting money was knocking nails into a piece of wood. Each nail raised a mark for the war effort.

GWHF16_230. Amateur flower-girls at the Caledonian market also raising money for the Wounded Allies' Relief Committee.

GWHF16_234. The same method was also used in Britain but the model was more *ad hoc*. British nurses, from Mile End, helped by wounded soldiers, knock nails into an effigy of the Kaiser on a ladder loaned by Harrods. This photograph was taken at Stepney borough fête, held to collect funds for wounded and disabled soldiers.

GWHF16_235. Money was not scarce in certain quarters. On 24 June the King inspected a convoy of motor ambulances presented to the French Army for use at Verdun. The members of Lloyd's had subscribed £40,000 for this purchase.

GWHF16_236. With more police being conscripted, the number of special constables increased. Colonel Sir Edward Ward, Permanent Secretary of the War Office, is inspecting special constables in London.

GWHF16_237. Lord French was in charge of Home Defence which more and more fell on those too old or unfit to serve. He is seen here taking the salute at a march past of the National Reserve.

GWHF16_238. In July 1916, the Princess Royal presented a flag and shield to the Australian Forces, gifts from British women and children. The ceremony took place at Wellington Barracks under the auspices of the League of Empire.

GWHF16_239. On 14 July, Paris turned out to give French, Russian, Belgian, and British troops a glorious welcome. President Poincaré presented diplomas, crosses and medals to the representatives of the first 500 officers who fell on the field of honour.

GWHF16_241. Highlanders marching during the 14 July celebrations.

GWHF16_240. Indian troops marching down the Champs Elysées during the 14 July celebrations.

GWHF16_242. Previous mention has been made and shown of the Portuguese entry into the war. The declaration of war against Germany was greeted with almost the same enthusiasm as the start of the war.

GWHF16_243. The Anzac contingent, marching in column to the commemoration service at Westminster Abbey on 25 April.

GWHF16_244. While still neutral, President Wilson headed a 'Preparedness Parade' on 24 June. A demonstration of preparedness for all eventualities.

GWHF16_245. The central London YMCA, a temporary home for many thousands of young men during the war whilst going on or coming from leave.

GWHF16_246. Thousands also stayed at smaller YMCA buildings, like this specially constructed Shakespeare hut in Gower Street.

GWHF16_247. A temporary YMCA accommodation hut at Aldwych.

GWHF16_248. The Aldwych hut was opened by Queen Alexandra. At the opening of the hut she personally served tea to a number of wounded men.

GWHF16_250. A shortage of porters caused by enlistment meant that passengers had to handle their own luggage.

GWHF16_249. The king is here seen inspecting men at the Inns of Court OTC camp.

GWHF16_252. Some sent their children during their dinner hour to collect their fuel.

GWHF16_251. With many delivery men serving with the colours, people had to collect their own coal.

GWHF16_253. Children in Britain and Germany were never close enough to the war to worry about gas, but in some front-line French towns a gas mask was an essential piece of clothing. These are French school children in Reims.

GWHF16_254. In Reims there was also the problem of the bombardment, so for many life went on underground. A subterranean classroom in Reims.

GWHF16_255. With a shortage of men and draught animals, anything went. A popular sight in Sheffield was an elephant pulling loads equivalent to five horses.

GWHF16_256. Camels also replaced horses, in this case to help with the ploughing.

GWHF16_260. The King's third son, aged 16 in 1916, Prince Henry was still at school when this photo of him in uniform was taken. He was not called up but was a member of the Eton College branch of the Officer Training Corps.

GWHF16_258. The fighting in Poland caused many thousands of Poles to flee to Russia. To help them, the Britain-to-Poland Fund needed money and sent representatives to help the situation.

GWHF16_257. As well as collecting money to help refugees some women volunteered to travel abroad to help them. This is the Women's Maternity Unit, organised by the National Union of Women's Suffrage Societies, at King's Cross leaving for Petrograd to aid refugees in Russia.

GWHF16_259. After losing the Russo-Japanese war, Russia was now an ally of her former enemy. A useful contribution Japan made was the sending of medical units to Europe where they worked in France. They also sent them to Russia. The photograph shows a Japanese Red Cross ambulance party of physicians and nurses departing for Russia.

GWHF16_262. The Berlin to Baghdad railway was started in 1903 and not completed until 1940. By 1916, with Bulgaria fighting with Germany and most of Serbia conquered, it was decided to run a train from Berlin to Constantinople – the *Balkanzug*. The first train left Berlin at 7.20 am on 15 January 1916 travelling via Dresden, Vienna, Belgrade, and Sofia. It was cheered enthusiastically along the route. On the inaugural voyage, the King of Saxony, Friedrich August III, travelled on it from Dresden to Tetschen in Bohemia.

GWHF16_261. Earl Kitchener's importance is shown by the locomotive in the photo. It is a GCR 4-6-0 mixed traffic locomotive built in December 1914, named Earl Kitchener of Khartoum. Here it is seen working sometime in 1916.

GWHF16_263/263a. Following on from the Germans introducing Daylight Savings Time, it was adopted by the British government. To inform the population, notices were put up by the government informing the public that on the night of Saturday 20/21 May at 2 am clocks would be put forward one hour. A German postcard advising the public of the time change that would happen on 1 May.

HF16_265. The name of this halt on the Stuartstown narrow-gauge railway in ...al, South Africa was originally *Himmelberg*. After Edith Cavell was executed, ...l never forget you and never forgive – Cavell' was chalked over the name. Later ...old board was taken down and a new one bearing the inscription on the photo took ...lace.

GWHF16_264. On Easter Monday, the Reverend E.N. Mellish had the ribbon of the Victoria Cross pinned on his chest by the divisional commander. It was awarded for his 'courage and devotion in succouring the wounded at St Eloi'. Here on leave on 4 June he is seen resuming his work as the curate of St Paul's, Deptford. He had served with Baden-Powell's police in South Africa and served during the South African war.

GWHF16_267. 'Men too old or unfit for service in the army volunteered for work in munition factories. They were trained in engineering schools and many of those who could not give their whole time to munitions put in long spells of work after office hours.'

GWHF16_266. A method of raising funds used in Britain and Germany was trench building. This faithful reproduction of front line trenches was dug in Heaton Park, Manchester, by convalescent soldiers. As well as showing civilians what the trenches were like, it was also to raise funds for soldiers and sailors that were blinded during the war.

GWHF16_268. In order to raise money during the war, the government asked people to invest in war loans with fixed interest over a fixed term. Each new loan was accompanied by a prospectus which these men have just got from the Bank of England. The purpose of the loan was both to fund the war and also to take money out of circulation and reduce inflation.

GWHF16_269. The 99th Essex County Reserve Battalion, Canadian Expeditionary Force, was mobilised in the city of Windsor, Ontario. Like many of the Canadian regiments they brought their colours with them to Britain and left them in churches for safe keeping. Their colours were deposited at the parish church of St John the Baptist, in High Street, Windsor, England. In the centre of the picture are the Mayor of Windsor and the battalion commander Lieutenant Colonel T.B. Welch.

GWHF16_270. The need for temporary hospitals was so great that even chapels were requisitioned by the army. One such building was the Wesleyan Chapel on Barry Island which became St John's Military Hospital. On one occasion it reverted to its original use and became a chapel for a day. A special day for Sapper W.H. Crockett RE and Miss Mitchell, staff, nurses and patients formed a 'guard of honour' outside the church.

GWHF16_271. As the Ministry of Munitions grew in size and importance it outgrew its original offices and new premises had to be found. The Hotel Metropole was taken over in 1916 and was still in use in 1919.

GWHF16_272. As oil had to be imported, and most was needed by the armed forces, there was little petrol to spare. A poster in Piccadilly advising against wasting precious fuel on having fun.

GWHF16_273. Sport was a way of keeping soldiers occupied when they were not training or in the trenches. It was healthy and enjoyable to watch. Sporting fixtures continued throughout the war. This one is in Germany and was watched by large crowds. The best soldier athletes competed against each other; most were probably glad to be back in Germany.

GWHF16_274. As well as the usual track and field events these German games had another competition: who could throw a grenade the furthest?

GWHF16_275. Football continued throughout the war, usually with soldiers and airmen based in the country or home on leave. This Paris match drew a very large crowd.

Section 8
Christmas

GWHF16_276. At the end of the year, people's thoughts turned to Christmas and the New Year, the season of parties. These young ladies in Hull are dressed to represent different nations for a New Year's party.

The Lord watch between me and thee, when we are absent one from another.

Christmas, 1916.

To ....

From ....

HOME WORDS NO. 165

BURNHAM CHURCH.

A GLIMPSE OF HOME WHERE YOU
ARE NOT FORGOTTEN

CHRISTMAS, 1916.

GWHF16_278. Many churches and organisations sent gifts to the men of the area at Christmas. The congregation of Burnham Church sent a card to each of the men from the parish who were serving with the colours.

GWHF16_280. The instructions at the top were very clear: if anything else was added, the Field postcard would be destroyed. But as it was Christmas, this, like many others from men who could not get a real card, was allowed through.

NOTHING is to be written on this side except the date and signature of the sender. Sentences not required may be erased. If anything else is added the post card will be destroyed.

I am quite well.

I have been admitted into hospital
{ sick } and am going on well.
{ wounded } and hope to be discharged soon.

I am being sent down to the base.

I have received your { letter dated _____
{ telegram „ _____
{ parcel „ _____

Letter follows at first opportunity.

I have received no letter from you
{ lately.
{ for a long time.

Signature only. } *ROS*

Date _____ 21·12·'16.

[Postage must be prepaid on any letter or post card addressed to the sender of this card.]

(98871) Wt. W3497-293 4.500m. 7·16 J. J. K. & Co., Ltd.

GWHF16_279. As in the two previous Christmases, cards arrived from all over the world. This was sent from Ireland where the battalion was helping to maintain the peace.

Wesleyan Methodist Church.

Christmas, 1916. :: New Year's Day, 1917.

AT this holy season the Wesleyan Methodist Church holds in loving remembrance all her absent sons, who, on land and sea, beneath the sea and in the air, are risking their lives for truth and honour, the freedom of the nations, and international righteousness. May He Who is our Joy grant them gladness. May He Who is our Strength in weakness comfort all who suffer, and ease their pain.

'May God's Peace keep guard over your hearts and minds in Christ Jesus' (Philippians iv. 7).

'No storm of earth shall keep afar
The peace that cannot turn to war.'

J. G. Tasker,
President of the Conference.

GWHF16_281. Economy in action. A Christmas and New Year card covered by one message.

1916 Home Front Timeline

January

1 First films about the Western Front released.

3 Clydeside Socialist newspaper *Forward* suppressed for four weeks.

4 Lord Derby's report on recruiting published; of the five million men of military age, just over half had offered themselves for enlistment.

5 Military Service Bill passed by Commons.

6 Statement on contraband in parcel mails to neutral countries published by Press Bureau.

7 Commons debate on the blockade.

8 Order in Council on control of shipping and a restriction of imports.
Board of Trade given the power to wind up enemy businesses.

9 Protest against closing of London museums. Labour conference decides to allow its members to remain in the cabinet.

11 Reichstag votes OAP age reduction from 70 to 65. Major strikes at Nikolayev, Black Sea Naval base, and Petrograd.

12 Canadian government votes to tax war profits at 25 per cent.

13 British government votes to raise Royal Navy to 350,000 men, an increase of 50,000.

20 First Derby scheme men called up.

22 German hit-and-run raids on Dover and Folkestone airship shed cause little damage.

23 Raids on Dover and Folkestone result in seven casualties.

27 First Military Service Act passed by House of Commons.

29 Prototype tank begins trials. Zeppelin raid on Paris causes fifty-four casualties.

30 War Savings Committees begun.

31 Nine Zeppelins raid West Suffolk and Midland Counties – 70 killed and 113 injured. Over 8,000 children exempted from school for farm work.

February

1 Food retail prices (RFP) 47 per cent over 1914 prices.

4 Whole of British coastline prohibited to enemy resident aliens.

7 Four Glasgow shop stewards arrested for conduct prejudicial to the war effort.

9 Air raid on Margate and Broadstairs – 3 injured. Extension of restrictions on lighting and on sale of sugar.

10   Military Service Act in force. Single men aged 19-30 called up for 3-17 March.

13   Paper shortage in Germany causes hundreds of periodicals to close.

14   Remaining classes of single men called up. To reduce manpower shortage in Turkey military service age increased to fifty with payment to government for those excused. Austrians bomb Milan and three other cities.

15   Speeches on the war by Mr Asquith and Lord Kitchener.

16   Air debate in the Commons.

18   Italians bomb Austrian town of Laibach in retaliation for Austrian attack on Milan on 14 February.

20   Aeroplane raid on Kent and East Suffolk – 1 killed and 1 injured.

21   Parliament votes on further credit – a supplementary £120 million, bringing the year's war votes to £1,420,000,000.

22   The House of Lords attacks the blockade policy. War Savings Certificates go on sale.

23   Lord Robert Cecil appointed Minister of Blockade. Peace debate in Commons.

26   German government orders a War Profits Tax.

29   Government recognises National Volunteer Force for Home Defence. Proclamation creates a blacklist of forbidden companies and people with which trade is expressly forbidden.

March

1   Aeroplane raid on Broadstairs and Margate – 1 killed. RFP 49 per cent.

2   Order in Council on Government of Ireland Act (1914). Lord Derby speaks in the Lords on recruiting – criticises system of exemptions; women must take the place of men. All single men aged 18-41 liable for call-up.

5   Zeppelin raid on Hull, East Riding, Lincolnshire, Leicestershire, Kent and Rutland – 18 killed and 52 injured.

6   Women's National Land Service Corps inaugurated. Quantity of material to be used for brewing reduced by 12½ per cent.

7   Prime Minister of Australia (Mr Hughes) arrives in England.

8   Special commission on commerce appointed.
    Air debate in the Lords, with Lord Montagu urging the setting up of an Air Board and advocating the production of more powerful machines and the construction of better anti-aircraft guns. In neutral America, the peace and quiet of Columbus, New Mexico was disrupted by an armed raid from Mexico. Pancho Villa raided the town and killed seventeen Americans. Germany declares war on Portugal.

14   Army estimates in Parliament allow for pensions for those discharged owing to illness contracted on service, with 4/5ths full pay if aggravated by service.

15   Lord Derby's pledge to married men with regard to military service. Board of Trade appeals for less meat consumption and household fuel economy.

16 South Wales coal dispute decided; miners must join recognised unions in order to maintain output.

18 Royal Defence Corps formed. Across Britain 3,078 factories involved in munitions manufacture.

17 Four seaplanes raid Dover, Ramsgate, Margate and Deal. Little material damage but 14 civilians killed and 26 wounded. One raider brought down at sea by Flight Commander Bone, RNAS.

18 Recruiting conference at War Office.

19 Disturbances at Tullamore, King's County. Loyalist crowds demonstrate against Sinn Fein premises, with police stopping the disturbance. Three police wounded by shots fired from Sinn Fein HQ. Four Irish volunteers arrested.

20 Central Tribunal for Great Britain set up.

21 General Cadorna received by King George.

22 Gaelic press offices in Dublin raided.

31 Army Council takes over hay and straw. Zeppelin raid on Lincolnshire, Essex and Suffolk – 48 killed and 64 injured. One intruder destroyed.

April

1   Zeppelin raid on County Durham and North Yorkshire – killed 22 and injured 130. Zeppelin L15 captured. King George presents £100,000 for war purposes. In Turkey, boys aged between 12 and 17 must join the Boy Scouts.

2   Powder explosion at Faversham in Kent causes 172 casualties, 106 deaths. Resumption of work advised by Clyde strike committee. Zeppelin raid on East Suffolk, Northumberland, London and Scotland – 13 killed and 24 injured. Thousands of men in Lille impressed to work for the Germans.

3   Zeppelin raid on Norfolk – no casualties.

4   Budget introduced with new taxes on amusements, matches and mineral waters. Income tax up to 5/- in the pound. Fifty to sixty per cent increase in taxes on sugar, cocoa, coffee, motorcars and excess profits. Zeppelin raid on East coast – 1 killed and 9 injured.

5   List of certified trades under Military Service Act revised. Zeppelin raid on Yorkshire and County Durham – 1 killed and 9 injured.

6   First married groups called up.

9   Asquith defines Allied position in a speech to French deputies visiting London. Lords Derby and Montagu resign from Air Committee.

11 Ludovico Zender, a German spy, shot in the Tower of London.

12 Clyde strikers tried for sedition.

16 Austrian government imposes War Profit Tax.

17 Committee appointed to investigate recruiting. Committee held that there was no case for

extension of Military Service Act to all men of military age, but suggested extension of the Act to include those reaching the age of 18, the retention of time-expired regulars, further combing-out of single men, and perseverance with existing methods of recruiting.

18 Lord Milner advocates universal military service in the House of Lords.

19 Cabinet crisis on manpower question reported. British weapon and chemical industries now employing 200,000 women.

20 New Volunteer regulations issued. Manpower proposals to be submitted to secret session of both Houses. Sir Roger Casement lands in Ireland and is arrested. Disguised German warship *Aud* sunk while trying to land arms on the Irish coast. French government fixes prices for food and coal and some commodities.

22 Easter manoeuvres of Sinn Fein volunteers cancelled.

24 Outbreak of the Irish Rebellion.

23 Zeppelin raid on Lincolnshire, Cambridgeshire, Norfolk and Suffolk – 1 killed and 1 injured. Aeroplane raid on Dover – no casualties. Rebellion in Ireland – Sinn Feiners seize Dublin Post Office; serious fighting in the streets of Dublin. Yarmouth and Lowestoft bombarded from sea by German cruiser squadron – 4 killed and 19 injured.

24 Martial law in Dublin. German battle cruiser squadron raids Lowestoft – engaged and dispersed by local naval forces. Great Yarmouth bombarded – 4 killed and 19 wounded. Zeppelin raid on East Suffolk, Kent, Essex and London – 1 person injured. German government signs a PoW exchange agreement with Britain. Men to pass through Switzerland.

25 Zeppelin raid on Kent – no damage caused.

26 Martial law across Ireland. General Sir J. Maxwell takes command in Ireland. New Military Service Bill abandoned.

30 Dublin Post Office burned by Irish nationalists. 707 Dublin rebels surrender.

May

1 End of Irish uprising. Zeppelin raid on Yorkshire, Northumberland and Scotland with 9 killed and 30 injured. Zeppelin L20 wrecked by storm off Norway. 10,000 Berlin workers protest against the war. RFP 55 per cent.

2 Aeroplane raid on Deal – 4 injured. Three Irish leaders shot. Mr Birrell resigns as Irish Secretary. Military Service Bill extending compulsion to married men is introduced.

5 Four Irish rebels shot.

8 Four more Irish rebels shot.

9 Appeal of Irish nationalists to support the constitutional movement. Duma (Russian parliament) members received by King George.

10 Commission appointed to enquire into the causes of the Irish rebellion.

11 Debate in Parliament on Irish administration. Mr Asquith announces the execution of twelve Irish rebels and that he would visit Ireland in the near future. In total 73 sentenced to penal servitude and 6 to imprisonment for life.
12 Mr Asquith visits Dublin. Juvenile crime on the increase.
13 In London British government sign PoW exchange with Germany.
14 Statement of war aims by Sir E. Grey. Sir Roger Casement charged with high treason.
15 Military Service Bill extending compulsion to married men passes the Commons.
16 Daylight Saving Bill passed. Air Board formed with Lord Curzon as President.
17 Royal Commission on Irish rebellion opens.
18 Air raid on Kent and Dover – 1 killed and 2 injured. One raider destroyed over the Belgian coast.
21 Daylight Savings Bill comes into operation.
22 Daily cost of the war recorded as £4,820,000.
23 Vote of credit for £300 million. Munitions workers' patriotic procession.
25 Military Service Act becomes law. Lloyd George undertakes settlement of the Irish question. According to the King's message to his people 5,031,000 have voluntarily enrolled since the start of the war.
28 London to Paris airmail service begins.
29 British civilian casualties in the war to date: 550 killed and 1,616 wounded.
31 Nearly 16,000 children exempt from school to work on farms.

June

5 HMS *Hampshire* mined off Scottish coast when proceeding to Russia: Lord Kitchener and his staff drowned – 75 bodies washed ashore, 12 survivors recovered. Non-Conscription Fellowship raided by police. Bertrand Russell fined and dismissed from Trinity College. RFP now 59 per cent above 1914 costs.
8 Compulsion replaces voluntary enlistment in Great Britain.
10 Compulsory Service Bill passed in New Zealand.
14 King George visits the Grand Fleet at Scapa.
18 War now costing Britain over £6 million a day.
19 A single French plane drops German war guilt leaflets on Berlin.
22 French bombers attack Karlsruhe causing 266 civilian casualties.
25 Trial of Sir Roger Casement begins.
26 Over 5,000 engineers working for Vickers in Barrow go on strike.
28 Three-day protest strikes over Liebknecht's two-year hard labour sentence for his involvement in anti-war protests. It is reported that 400 German firms are still trading in Britain.
29 Sir Roger Casement found guilty of high treason and sentenced to death.
30 French government increases alcohol duties.

July

1   Walkers on Hampstead Heath claim to hear the Somme barrage. Over 750,000 women working in industry and commerce. RFP 61 per cent above 1914 costs.

3   Barrow strike called off. First free market on the Stock Exchange.

4   Ignatius Tribbitch Lincoln, ex-MP, sentenced to three years in prison for forgery.

6   Lloyd George becomes Secretary of State for War, with Lord Derby as Under Secretary. Hospital ships land at Dover and Southampton; over 10,000 men wounded during the Somme battle.

7   King George sends a message of congratulation to the troops in France.

8   Order in Council rescinds Declaration of London of 25 February 1909. E.S. Montagu appointed as Minister of Munitions. Two German aeroplane raids on southeast coast (Dover and North Foreland) with no damage.

10   German submarine shells Seaham Harbour killing one women. Three armed trawlers sunk off Scottish coast in action with German submarines.

13   Bank Holiday suspended. Allied conference on munitions output held in London. Bank rate 6 per cent. German submarine sinks two trawlers and two fishing boats off Whitby.

16   Start of War Savings Week.

17   Trade Unions recommend postponement of all holidays in connection with munitions production. 'Munitionettes' rate of pay fixed at 4½d per hour if aged over 18.

22   Silver badge granted for those disabled while serving in the armed forces. General Maxwell's despatches on Irish rebellion published in *The Times*.

24   Vote of Credit for £450 million moved in Commons.

27   Captain Charles Fryatt of the Great Eastern Liner *Brussels* is court-martialled and shot by German authorities in Belgium for attempting to ram a German submarine. Central tribunal reports 4,378 genuine conscientious objectors

28   Zeppelin raid on Lincolnshire and Norfolk – no casualties. Prime Minister in House of Commons denounces murder of Captain Fryatt. Government contemplates immediate action. H.E. Drake becomes Chief Secretary for Ireland.

30   Munitions explosion on Black Tom Island near New York causes $40million damage; found to have been caused by sabotage.

31   Unpredicted winds disperse 8 airships that drop 103 bombs over 6 counties causing no casualties.

August

1   RFP 60 per cent; the first fall since August 1914. Petrol rationing to start.

3   Prime Minister receives deputation from miners, railway men and transport workers for discussions about demobilisation problems after the war. Zeppelin raid on Norfolk, East Suffolk and Kent – no damage. Sir Roger Casement hanged at Pentonville prison.

4   Army releases 27,000 men to help with the harvest.
7   Admiralty deny allegation in German press that British Hospital ships are being used as troop transports. August Bank Holiday postponed.
8   Zeppelin raid over Eastern England and Scotland. Of 173 bombs dropped, the most damage is done in Hull where two are killed and a further twenty injured.
9   Zeppelin raid on northern counties and Norfolk – 10 killed and 16 injured.
10 Mr McKenna submits a balance sheet to the Commons, based on the war continuing until 31 March 1917 – the country would be indebted by £3,440,000,000 with a national income of up to £2,640,000,000. Premiere of the film *Battle of the Somme* at the Scala Theatre, London.
11 Seaplane raid on Dover – seven injured.
17 In Germany the meat ration is fixed.
18 Appeals made to munition workers not to take holidays.
19 Coal miners in the Ruhr strike against food shortages and inflation.
22 Lloyd George gives survey of military situation and announces thirty-five Zeppelins destroyed by the Allies.
23 Army Zeppelin (LZ97) raid on East Suffolk – no casualties.
24 Zeppelin raid on East Suffolk, Essex, Kent and London – 9 killed and 40 injured.
25 Zeppelin raid on East and Southeast coast and London.

September

1   Turkish planes bomb Port Said injuring forty-six. RFP now 65 per cent. War Propaganda Bureau starts production of monthly magazine, *War Pictorial*. Munitions workers total 640,000 men and women, in 4,212 factories but only 435 canteens provided so far.
3   Thirteen airships raid the Midlands and North Home Counties, Kent and London, 4 killed and 13 injured. Lieutenant William Leefe Robinson awarded VC for shooting down German airship over Cuffley, near Enfield.
4   TUC at Birmingham demands full rights back after the war and protests against cost of living and the military control of labour.
5   Mr Balfour speaks to local Glasgow trade unions about shipyard labour.
9   In Cardiff, South Wales railwaymen resolve to strike, demanding an increase of 10/- weekly on wages. Austrian War Minister warns of malnutrition in the army and government ministers discuss food shortages.
20 Railway workers given 5s/week extra after strike. Women get extra 3s/week war wage.
22 Aeroplane raid on Kent and Dover – no damage.
23 Big raid by German airships (probably twelve) on London, Lincolnshire, Nottinghamshire, Norfolk and Kent. Two airships brought down, one in flames. The second Zeppelin set fire by the crew before they surrendered; casualties due to the raid were 40 killed and 130 injured.

25   Seven airships raid Lancashire, Yorkshire and Lincolnshire – 43 killed and 31 injured.
30   Enemy banks wound up, releasing £58.8 million to government.

October

1   Airship L31 brought down at Potter's Bar after raid on the Midlands and north Home
     Counties, Hertfordshire and London – 1 killed and 1 injured. Munitions holiday to replace
     Whitsuntide and August Bank holidays. RFP 68 per cent.
3   Belgian unemployed to be forced to work in Germany.
4   Women offered free munitions work training.
5   French War Loan raises ten billion francs.
6   Scheme for unfit soldiers to go into agriculture.
8   Prohibition of Sunday munitions work.
11   Mr Asquith delivers speech on 'No patched-up peace'.
12   Army Reserve Munitions Workers Scheme begun to release unskilled workers aged under
     30.
13   Worst month for strikes in Russia: 189 strikes, over ninety per cent political, involve nearly
     200,000 workers.
15   Board of Trade issues average increase in retail prices of principal food articles between
     July 1914 and September 1916; average increase, 65 per cent.
18   In Britain men aged 41 called up.
22   Aeroplane raid on Sheerness – 2 injured.
23   Aeroplane raid on Margate – no injuries.
24   15,000 deported Belgians working in Germany. Ministry of Munitions to pay seventy-five
     per cent of cost of temporary crèches for children of married women workers.
26   Raising of military age to 60 opposed by German Chancellor, Bethmann-Hollweg.
28   British and German governments agree to exchange interned civilians aged over 45.
     German government drafts compulsory service bill for males aged 15 to 60 which is
     adopted on 21 November.
30   Early closing in British shops: 6pm Monday to Friday, 9pm Saturday.
31   Increased wages demanded by Cardiff miners.

November

1   Cardiff Peace Conference broken up by patriotic mob. RFP 78 per cent.
5   Guy Fawkes Night cancelled.
9   Shortage of boys impairs delivery of telegrams.
13   Mata Hari interrogated at Scotland Yard but she is sent back to Spain.
14   Pensions Bill introduced.

15 Appointment of Food Controller. In Germany the Class of 1918, all under 19 years old, begin to join the army for training.

16 Strike by 12,000 Sheffield engineers results in colleagues' release from HM forces.

17 Food regulations issued; Board of Trade invested with wide powers to prevent waste, regulate manufacture and production, direct sale and distribution, control markets, regulate price and commandeer any article.

19 50,000 deported Belgian workers now in Germany.

21 Emperor Franz Joseph of Austria-Hungary dies and is succeeded by his great-nephew Charles.

20 Milk and flour regulations issued by Board of Trade.

23 German destroyers raid in the Channel at the north end of the Downs – little damage.

26 German naval raid near Lowestoft – armed trawler *Narval* sunk.

27 Zeppelin raid on Durham, Yorkshire, Staffordshire and Cheshire – two raiders brought down – 4 killed and 37 injured.

28 One aeroplane raids London at midday injuring ten people. The aeroplane was subsequently shot down in France. Brixham fishing fleet attacked by German submarine.

29 The Board of Trade to take over the South Wales coalfield from 1 December.

30 Lord Derby speaks on conditions for the New Volunteer Army – no man to lose civil employment and no compulsion to sign agreement, not to leave home save for defence of country. Franz Joseph's funeral attended by the Kaiser, Tsar Ferdinand of Bulgaria, the Kings of Bavaria and Saxony, the Crown Princes of Germany, Sweden and Turkey. 15,000 Manchester engineers begin strike against low wage award.

December

1 Lloyd George states he is unable to remain in government because of his dissatisfaction with the leisurely conduct of the war. Women's Army Auxiliary Corps formed to help release men for the army. RFP stands at 84 per cent.

3 Asquith decides on reconstruction of government. Wage dispute in South Wales settled in favour of miners.

4 Lloyd George resigns.

5 Asquith resigns. In Germany the Auxiliary Service Law makes all males aged 17 to 60 liable for service. An explosion at Barnbow munitions factory near Leeds kills thirty-five munitionettes.

6 Cabinet crisis – Lloyd George asked to form administration. The Board of Agriculture is given powers to acquire land.

6 Lloyd George becomes Prime Minister. Call up of non-skilled munition workers agreed.

9 New War Cabinet formed and meets for first time. Ministries of Food, Labour and Shipping formed.

11 Grey resigns as British Foreign Secretary. Ministry of Labour comes into being. Lord Derby succeeds Lloyd George as War Minister.

14 House of Commons asked for fifth Vote of Credit in the financial year – a further £400 million; total cost £1,950 million.

16 Government decides to take over Irish railways, to the satisfaction of the Irish people.

17 German peace note received by the Foreign Office which lays the blame for the continuation of the war upon the Allied governments.

19 Lloyd George's first speech as Prime Minister calls for the control of shipping, mining and food.

22 Ministries of food, pensions and shipping formed and the Air Board becomes the Air Ministry. King George's speech to Parliament urges the vigorous prosecution of the war until the security of Europe is firmly established.

31 Total air raid casualties for the year, 311 killed and 752 injured. In final quarter of the year the tonnage of neutral shipping entering British ports is less than a third on the first quarter's tonnage: 959,000 as compared to 3,442,000.

Bibliography, Sources and Further Reading

Baer, C.H. *Der Völkerkreig*. Volumes 11 to 21. Julius Hoffmann. 1917.

British Food Policy during the First World War. Allen & Unwin. 1985.

Becker, J. *The Great War and the French People*. Berg. 1990.

Bilton, D. *Hull in the Great War*. Pen & Sword. 2015.

Bilton, D. *Reading in the Great War*. Pen & Sword. 2015.

Bilton, D. *The Home Front in the Great War – Aspects of Conflict*. Leo Cooper.   2003.

Charman, I. *The Great War, The People's Story*. Random House. 2014.

Chickering, R. *Imperial Germany and the Great War, 1914-1918*. Cambridge University Press. 2005.

Fridenson, P. (Ed.) *The French Home Front, 1914-1918*. Berg. 1992.

Gregory, A. *The Last Great War. British Society and the First World War*. Cambridge University Press. 2008.

Hastings, M. *Catastrophe*. William Collins. 2013.

Herwig, H.H. *The First World War. Germany and Austria-Hungary 1914-1918*. Arnold. 1997.

Horn, P. *Rural Life in England in the First World War*. Gill and MacMillan. 1984.

Kennedy, R. *The Children's War*. Palgrave Macmillan. 2014.

Kocka, J. *Facing Total War. German Society 1914-1918*. Berg. 1984.

Markham, J. *Keep the Home Fires Burning*. Highgate Publications. 1988

Martin, C. *English Life in the First World War*. Wayland. 1974.

Marwick, A. *The Deluge. British Society and the First World War*. Macmillan. 1973.

Marwick, A. *Women at War*. Fontana. 1977.

McGrandle, L. *The Cost of Living in Britain*. Wayland. 1974.

Reetz, W. *Eine ganze Welt gegen uns*. Ullstein. 1934.

Rex, H. *Der Weltkrieg in seiner Rauhen wirklichkeit*. Hermann Rutz. 1926.

Stein, W. Um *Vaterland und Freiheit*. Volumes 2 and 3. Hermann Montanus. 1915.

The Berkshire Chronicle.

The Hull Times.

The Hull Daily Mail.

The Reading Standard.

Turner, E.S. *Dear Old Blighty*. Michael Joseph. 1980.

Unknown. *Grosser Bilder Atlas des Weltkrieges*. Bruckemann. 1916.

Unknown. *History of the War*. Volumes 10 to 12. The Times. 1916.

Unknown. *The Illustrated War News*. Illustrated London News and Sketch, Ltd., 1916.

Unknown. *Illustrated London News*. January – December 1916. Illustrated London News and Sketch Ltd., 1916.

Unknown. *Kamerad im Westen*. Societäts-Verlag/Frankfurt am Main. 1930.

Various. *Thuringen im und nach dem Weltkrieg*. Lippold. 1920.

Williams, J. *The Home Fronts*. Constable & Co Ltd. 1972.

Winter, J.M. *The Experience of World War 1*. Equinox (Oxford) Ltd. 1986.

Winter, J. *The First World War*. Volume III. Civil Society. Cambridge University Press. 2014.

Wilson, H.W. (Ed.) *The Great War. The Standard History of the All Europe Conflict*. Volumes 6 to 8. Amalgamated Press 1916.

Index